Human Rights Law and Practice

Human Rights Law and Practice

Supplement to the First Edition

GENERAL EDITORS

Lord Lester of Herne Hill
QC, MA (Cantab), LLM (Harvard), President of International Centre for the Legal
Protection of Human Rights, of Lincoln's Inn, Barrister

David Pannick
QC, MA (Oxon), BCL (Oxon), Gray's Inn, Barrister, Fellow of All Souls College,
Oxford

CONTRIBUTORS

Monica Carss-Frisk LLB (Lond), BCL (Oxon), of Gray's Inn, Barrister

Brice Dickson BA, BCL, MPhil, Barrister

Emma Dixon BA (Cantab), of Gray's Inn, Barrister

Ben Emmerson QC, LLB (Bristol), of Middle Temple, Barrister

Kate Gallafent BA (Cantab), of Gray's Inn, Barrister

Joanna Harrington BA (UBC), LLB (UVictoria), Barrister and Solicitor
(British Columbia)

Javan Herberg LLB (Lond), BCL (Oxon), of Lincoln's Inn, Barrister

Thomas de la Mare BA (Oxon) LLM (European University Institute), of
Middle Temple, Barrister

The Hon Lord Reed LLB (Edin), D Phil (Oxon), Senator of the College of
Justice in Scotland

Dinah Rose BA (Oxon), of Gray's Inn, Barrister

Pushpinder Saini MA (Oxon), BCL (Oxon), of Gray's Inn, Barrister

Mark Shaw BA (Dunelm), LLM (Cantab), of Inner Temple, Barrister

Butterworths
London, Edinburgh, Dublin
2000

United Kingdom	Butterworths, a Division of Reed Elsevier (UK) Ltd, Halsbury House, 35 Chancery Lane, London WC2A 1EL and 4 Hill Street, Edinburgh EH2 3JZ
Australia	Butterworths, a Division of Reed International Books Australia Pty Ltd, Chatswood, New South Wales
Canada	Butterworths Canada Ltd, Markham, Ontario
Hong Kong	Butterworths Asia (Hong Kong), Hong Kong
India	Butterworths India, New Delhi
Ireland	Butterworth (Ireland) Ltd, Dublin
Malaysia	Malayan Law Journal Sdn Bhd, Kuala Lumpur
New Zealand	Butterworths of New Zealand Ltd, Wellington
Singapore	Butterworths Asia, Singapore
South Africa	Butterworths Publishers (Pty) Ltd, Durban
USA	Lexis Law Publishing, Charlottesville, Virginia

© Reed Elsevier (UK) Ltd 2000
Reprinted 2001

A CIP Catalogue record for this book is available from the British Library.

ISBN 0 406 932 31X

LAW

Typeset by Doyle & Co, Colchester.
Printed by Hobbs, the Printers, Totton, Hampshire.

Visit Butterworths LEXIS *direct* at: http://www.butterworths.com

Preface

Life was much easier for lawyers who practised 'according to the law of the Medes and Persians, which altereth not'.[1] By contrast, human rights law is far from static. Indeed, it is one of the proudest boasts of the European Court of Human Rights that the European Convention on Human Rights 'is a living instrument' which evolves to meet the challenges, and the needs, of a developing society.[2]

There is, therefore, no rest for authors of a textbook on human rights.

The bringing into force on 2 October 2000 of the main provisions of the Human Rights Act 1998[3] is an appropriate moment to bring up to date the developments in this area of the law since we completed work on the first edition of this work.

Lord Lester of Herne Hill QC and David Pannick QC
Blackstone Chambers,
Temple,
London EC4Y 9BW
August 2000

---

1   Daniel, chapter 6, verse 8.
2   *Tyrer v United Kingdom* (1978) 2 EHRR 1 at 10, E Ct HR, para 31.
3   Human Rights Act 1998 (Commencement No 2) Order 2000, (SI 2000/1851) with effect from 12 July 2000.

Contents

Table of Statutes

Table of Statutory Instruments

Table of European Legislation

Table of International Legislation

Table of Cases

A

B

C

D

E

F

R

S

T

U

V

W

X

Y

Z

Chapter 1
History and context

1.45 [*Contd*] During the hiatus between Royal Assent (9 November 1998) and the coming into force of the main provisions of the Human Rights Act 1988 (HRA 1998), a wide range of implementing measures have been introduced.

1.46 Since Royal Assent, in accordance with HRA 1998, s 19, the Minister in charge of every Bill has issued a statement on the face of the Bill as to whether or not the Bill's provisions are, in the Minister's view, compatible with the Convention rights[1]. With a single exception, in each case the Minister has been able to make a statement that the provisions of the Bill are compatible with the Convention rights. However, when the Local Government Bill was introduced in the Commons on 13 March 2000, the Secretary of State for the Environment, Transport and the Regions included a statement under s 19(1)(b) that he was unable to say that in his view the Bill was compatible, but that the Government nevertheless wished the Commons to proceed with the Bill. The reason for this was that the Lords (where the Bill was first introduced) had amended the Bill to prevent the repeal of s 2A of the Local Government Act 1986, which appeared to be incompatible with the Convention rights to freedom of expression and to respect for private life in relation to homosexuals. The Minister explained[2] that there are 'considerable doubts whether section 2A ... is compatible.... Clause 91 of the Local Government Bill amends, but also reaffirms, the provisions of section 2A. It is for this reason that it is doubtful whether the Bill is compatible with the ECHR.'

1   The scrutiny arrangements for Scottish legislation, under the SA 1998, are described in paras **5.24–5.28**; for Northern Ireland Assembly legislation, under the NI Act 1998, are described in paras **6.23–6.31**, and for Welsh secondary legislation, under the GWA 1998, are described in para **7.06**.
2   Written Answer by Hilary Armstrong MP, Minister of State, Department of the Environment, Transport and the Regions, HC Official Record (6th Series) (23 March 2000), 624W.

1.47 Section 19 of the HRA 1998 applies only to primary legislation. However, the Government has decided[1] that 'a Minister inviting Parliament to approve a draft statutory instrument or statutory instrument subject to affirmative resolution should always volunteer his or her view regarding its compatibility with the Convention rights. The Minister's view should also always be given regarding the incompatibility of any secondary legislation to the extent that it amends primary legislation; and that statement should be made in writing where the secondary legislation which amends primary legislation is not subject to affirmative resolution. The written statement should be made in whatever form seems appropriate, for example in a letter to the Joint Select Committee on Statutory Instruments'.

1   Letter from the Legislation Clerk of the Home Office to the Clerk of the House of Lords Select Committee on Delegated Powers and Deregulation, in Annex 6 to the Select Committee's Report of 1 December 1999 (Session 1999–2000, 1st Report); see also 608 HL Official Report (5th series) (10 January 2000) WA 76.

1.48 Guidance produced by the Home Office Human Rights Unit aims to ensure that a common approach is taken across government in respect of compatibility statements[1]. If a statement under s 19(1)(a) is to be made, then the Minister must be clear that, at a minimum, the balance of argument supports the view that the provisions are compatible. This view is to be formed on the basis of appropriate legal advice as whether it is more likely than not that the provisions of the Bill will stand up to challenge on Convention grounds before the domestic courts and the Strasbourg Court. The existence of valid arguments that could be advanced against any anticipated challenge is not a sufficient basis to advise the making of a compatibility statement, if it is thought that these arguments would not ultimately succeed before the courts.

1 'Section 19 Process' (January 2000) Human Rights Unit, Home Office.

1.49 As regards the disclosure of the reasons for making a s 19 compatibility statement, the Government believes[1] that 'a Minister in charge of a Bill should be ready to address Convention related issues during proceedings, but the Minister must retain the discretion to decide how to do so in the context of the debate'. The Government also believes[2] that 'a debate in Parliament provides the best forum in which the person responsible can explain his or her thinking on the compatibility of the provisions of a Bill with the Convention rights. Reasons can then be given in the context of particular concerns about particular provisions. Convention issues are frequently complex. It would be difficult to do justice to them in a written statement accompanying a Bill and it would not be practical to provide a written statement of reasons in advance of the parliamentary proceedings on the Bill'.

1 612 HL Official Report (5th series) (20 March 2000), WA 8.
2 600 HL Official Report (5th series) (9 May 1999), WA 35.

1.50 The Home Office guidance given to Government Departments[1] emphasises that a Minister in charge of a Bill should be ready in a debate to explain his or her thinking on compatibility with respect to particular provisions, by giving a general outline of the arguments which have led him or her to reach the conclusion reflected in the s 19 statement. The guidance also notes that, although it would not normally be appropriate to disclose to Parliament the legal advice to Ministers, officials should ensure that Ministers are briefed in such a way as to enable them at least to identify the Convention points considered and the broad lines of the argument. However, so far no consistent practice has developed of Ministers giving sufficient reasons to explain the basis for their s 19 statements. It is to be hoped that there will be more consistent and fuller disclosure of reasons when the Joint Parliamentary Select Committee on Human Rights is fully operational.

1 'Section 19 Process' (January 2000) Human Rights Unit, Home Office, see para **1.48** above.

Human Rights: Joint Committee

1.51 The terms of reference of the Joint Select Committee on Human Rights have been published and agreed by Parliament. The terms are as follows:

(1) That it is expedient that a Joint Committee of Lords and Commons be appointed to consider and report on:
  (a) matters relating to human rights in the United Kingdom (but excluding consideration of individual cases);
  (b) proposals for remedial orders, draft remedial orders and remedial orders made under Section 10 of and laid under Schedule 2 to the Human Rights Act 1998; and
  (c) in respect of draft remedial orders and remedial orders, whether the special attention of the House should be drawn to them on any of the grounds specified in Standing Order 73 (Joint Committee on Statutory Instruments);
(2) to report to the House:
  (a) in relation to any document containing proposals laid before the House under paragraph 3 of the said Schedule 2, its recommendation whether a draft order in the same terms as the proposals should be laid before the House; or
  (b) in relation to any draft order laid under paragraph 2 of the said Schedule 2, its recommendation whether the draft order should be approved;
  and to have power to report to the House on any matter arising from its consideration of the said proposals or draft orders; and
(3) to report to the House in respect of any original order laid under paragraph 4 of the said Schedule 2, its recommendation whether:
  (a) the order should be approved in the form in which it was originally laid before Parliament; or
  (b) that the order should be replaced by a new order modifying the provisions of the original order; or
  (c) that the order should not be approved,
  and to have power to report to the House on any matter arising from its consideration of the said order or any replacement order.

1.52 Specific legislation has been introduced to give further effect to the Convention rights[1], and issues have been raised about the compatibility of provisions of draft and actual Bills with the Convention rights[2].

1   Eg, the Armed Forces (Discipline) Bill; the Regulation of Investigatory Powers Bill; and the Sexual Offences (Amendment) Bill.
2   Eg, the draft and actual Financial Services and Markets Bill; the Local Government Bill; and the Terrorism Bill.

1.53 A wide range of administrative measures has been taken by central government Departments and other public authorities in preparation for the coming into force of the main provisions of the HRA 1998. A Human Rights Task Force has been created, whose members include representatives from the Home Office, the Lord Chancellor's Department, the Cabinet Office, the Crown Prosecution Service, and non-governmental organisations, including JUSTICE, Liberty, Charter 88, the Human Rights Incorporation Project and the Institute for Public Policy Research[1]. A liaison group includes representatives of the Bar Council, the Law Society, the Scottish, Welsh and Northern Irish Executives and the Northern Ireland Human Rights Commission. The terms of reference of this Task Force include helping public authorities prepare for the implementation of the HRA 1998, and increasing general awareness of Convention rights and helping to 'build a human rights culture in the United Kingdom'[2]. The Task Force has assisted in reviewing procedures across the entire spectrum of government.

1   Minutes and agenda are available on the Home Office website www.homeoffice.gov.uk/hract.
2   'Task Force Terms of Reference', Home Office, available at www.homeoffice.gov.uk/hract/taskref.htm.

1.54   General guidance to civil servants dealing with HRA issues has been made available[1]. The Home Office Human Rights Unit has produced guidance for public authorities affected by the Act[2]. This sets out the key provisions of the HRA, and describes the areas of activity in which the Act may have an impact. The guidance also identifies some of the key characteristics of a public authority, to assist bodies in determining whether the HRA applies to their activities. These include:

(1) whether the body performs or operates in the public domain as an integral part of a statutory system which performs public law duties;

(2) whether the duty performed is of public significance;

(3) whether the rights or obligations of individuals may be affected in a performance of a duty;

(4) whether an individual may be deprived of some legitimate expectation in performance of a duty; and

(5) whether the body is non-statutory, but is established under the authority of government or local government.

The Department for Trade, Industry and the Regions and the Local Government Association have issued guidance to local authorities and have had discussions with other government departments, in particular, the Department of Health and the Department of Education and Employment. Guidance is to be given by the Lord Chancellor's Department and the Cabinet Office to ombudsmen about the application of Article 6 of the Convention to their procedures.

1   See *Judge Over Your Shoulder*, available at www.open.gov.uk/tsd/judge.htm.
2   *Core Guidance for Public Authorities – A New Era of Rights and Responsibilities*, available at www.homeoffice.gov.uk/hract/coregd.htm.

1.55   Between January and July 2000, the Judicial Studies Board for England and Wales provided training on the HRA 1998 for some 3000 full- and part-time judges at a one-day seminar, including 200 legally qualified tribunal Chairmen. The Lord Chancellor's Department has also worked with the Judicial Studies Board and the Magistrates' Courts Committees to develop training for lay magistrates, their legal advisers and other staff working in the magistrates' courts. 30, 000 lay magistrates have been provided with general awareness training[1].

1   See further Paul Ashcroft et al, *Human Rights and the Courts: Bringing Justice Home* (1999), published by members of the working group responsible for the training of magistrates and their legal advisers.

1.56   The Lord Chief Justice has chaired a working group of senior judges and officials, considering how senior judges should best be deployed to deal with the additional workload occasioned by the HRA 1998, and the arrangements needed to be set up within the Royal Courts of Justice to ensure that judgments are disseminated speedily to courts at first instance.

1.57   In Scotland, the Scottish Parliament and Scottish Executive have been required y the Scotland Act 1998 to act compatibly with the Convention Rights, as explained more fully in Chapter 5. Within the Scottish Executive, a Working Group has co-ordinated two ECHR Reviews across all departments. A detailed audit has also been carried out to identify potential ECHR challenges and the changes which may be necessary as a result. Specific legislation has been introduced in a number of areas where there was thought to be at least a serious risk of incompatibilty[1]. A range of administrative measures have also been taken, including participation by the Scottish Executive Justice Department in the Home Office Human Rights Task Force, participation by the Crown Office in Whitehall ECHR Criminal Issues Group and the issue y the Scottish Office of guidance on Human Rights in Scotland. The Scottish Executive has also announced its intention to carry out a consultation exercise on the question whether Scotland should establish a Human Rights Commission.

1   Eg the Bail, Judicial Appointments, Etc (Scotland) Bill and the Regulations of Investigatory Powers (Scotland) Bill.

1.58 On implementation of the HRA in Northern Ireland, see the updating material on chapter 6 below.

1.59 On implementation of the HRA in Wales, see the updating material on chapter 7 below.

1.60 In the Channel Islands and the Isle of Man, legislation has been introduced to incorporate the ECHR into the domestic law of these dependant territories. The Human Rights (Jersey) Law 2000 received the Royal Assent on 17 May. In Guernsey, the States of Deliberation approved a motion proposing the introduction of similar legislation on 5 April, and this legislation is expected to be introduced shortly. The Isle of Man's Human Rights Bill received its Second Reading in the House of Keys on 9 May 2000, and both this Bill and the Guernsey legislation are expected to receive the Royal Assent before the end of 2000[1].

1   613 HL Official Report (5th series) (24 May 2000) WA 90.

1.61 Following the friendly settlement reached in *Faulkner v United Kingdom*[1], the States of Guernsey is expected to legislate in late 2000 to establish a civil legal aid system in Guernsey[2].

1   (2000) Times, 11 January, E Ct HR.
2   612 HL Official Report (5th series) WA 115 (19 April 2000).

1.62 The UN Human Rights Committee in its Concluding Observations on the UK Dependant Territories Reports delivered in March 2000 under the International Covenant on Civil and Political Rights reporting procedure welcomed alterations in the law of the territories, in particular the various steps taken in all territories to combat any discrimination on the basis of sex and race[1]. The Committee went on to urge the UK to ensure that all Covenant rights are given effect in the domestic law of the territories, and that human rights education be extended to members of the police forces, the legal profession and other persons involved in the administration of justice, with a view to making it a part of their regular training. The Committee also recommended that the authorities in Guernsey and the Isle of Man give due consideration to establishing independent bodies with a mandate to review administrative decisions, and that legislation be introduced to outlaw corporal punishment in the Isle of Man. The Committee also urged the Jersey authorities to consider amending legislation to enable a withdrawal of the reservation to art 11 of the Covenant. Their conclusions also called for the authorities in the territories to provide for anti- terrorism laws that would comply with art 9 of the Covenant, and to take measures to remove and prohibit any discrimination on grounds of sexual orientation. The Committee noted with concern that the archaic and discriminatory provisions of the Criminal Code which make blasphemy a misdemeanor are still in force on the Isle of Man, and recommended that these be repealed. Further recommendations included that the territories introduce legislation and other effective measures to prohibit discrimination between women and men, that the authorities complete the current process of enacting legislation outlawing all racial discrimination and promulgate legislation prohibiting any discrimination, and that all persons are guaranteed equal and effective protection against discrimination on any ground such as race, colour, sex, language, religion, political or other opinion, national or social origin, property, birth or other status.

1　Concluding Observations of the Human Rights Committee, 27/03/2000 (CCPR/C/79/Add 119).The Committee in particular noted with appreciation the information provided by the delegation that all distinctions based on sex had been abolished with regard to inheritance of realty in Sark. The Committee also welcomed the steps taken in Jersey to eliminate differences between the rights of children born in wedlock and the rights of those born out of wedlock.

1.63 During the period since the HRA 1998 received Royal Assent (on 9 November 1998) the courts have made significant use of the Convention in construing legislation, deciding applications for judicial review of administrative decisions, and declaring the common law. Many of these decisions will continue to be relevant when the HRA 1998 is fully in force (on 2 October 2000).

1.64 In *R v DPP, ex p Kebilene*[1], the House of Lords decided that, since Parliament had expressly provided that the main provisions of the HRA 1998 were to take effect not on enactment but on the date specified by the Secretary of State (2 October 2000), it would be contrary to the legislative intention if those provisions were treated as though they had immediate effect. Accordingly, the Act did not give rise to a legitimate expectation that, prior to its taking full effect, the Director of Public Prosecutions would exercise his discretion to consent to a prosecution, for an alleged offence in breach of s 16A of the Prevention of Terrorism (Temporary Provisions) Act 1989, in accordance with the right to be presumed innocent, guaranteed by art 6(2) of the Convention. As regards the discretionary area of judgment, Lord Hope of Craighead approved (at 994b–d) the passage at para **3.21** of this work. Lord Hope also observed (at 988f–g) that when the HRA 1998 is in force, a generous and purposive construction should be given to its provisions in considering the compatibility of domestic legislation and acts of public authorities with the fundamental rights and freedoms enshrined in the Convention. This approach was applied when the case was returned for trial to the Central Criminal Court. Judge Pownall QC construed s 16A so as to be compatible with art 6(2) of the Convention by requiring the prosecution to discharge the ultimate burden of proof to the requisite criminal standard[2]. The prosecution was unable to do so and the trial was aborted. Subsequently to this, similar provisions in the Terrorism Bill (which extends many of the provisions of the Northern Ireland terrorism legislation throughout the UK and makes these counter-terrorist powers permanent) were amended during the Bill's passage through Parliament to establish clearly that the legal burden of proof ultimately rested with the prosecution.

1 [1999] 3 WLR 972.
2 *R v Kebiline* (Central Criminal Court, 14 February 2000, unreported).

1.65 In *R v Stratford Justices, ex p Imbert*[1], the Divisional Court (Buxton LJ and Collins J) held that, although the HRA 1998 was not in force and the Convention did not have any direct effect, the court could, in deciding whether a prosecution should be stayed as an abuse of process, have regard to art 6 of the Convention and its case law. Buxton LJ observed that in the present state of English law the Convention jurisprudence can be no more than one factor in the court's judgment. However, when the Act enters into force the court will have an obligation to make a careful enquiry into what the terms and limits of the relevant Convention right in fact are.

1 [1999] 2 Cr App Rep 276.

1.66 In *Brown v Stott*, the High Court of Justiciary, sitting as the Court of Criminal Appeal, decided that the Procurator Fiscal had no power to lead and rely on evidence of an admission which the appellant was compelled to make under s 172(2)(a) of the Road Traffic Act 1988 that she had been the driver of a motor car at the relevant time. The appellant had been subject to compulsion when she made an incriminating reply under threat of being found guilty of an offence and being punished with a fine. The Crown proposed to use evidence of the answer given by her as a significant part of the prosecution case against her at her trial. After a detailed analysis of the Convention and comparative constitutional case law, the Court held that the use the Crown proposed to make of her answer would offend her right not to incriminate herself, which is a constituent of fair procedure inherent in art 6(1) of the Convention. Section 172 was 'read down' and given effect in a way compatible with the appellant's Convention rights to silence and not to incriminate herself, by holding that it did not permit the Crown to lead and rely on evidence of her incriminating reply at her trial.

1 2000 SCCR 314.

1.67 In *Starrs v Ruxton*[1], the High Court of Justiciary, sitting as the Court of Criminal Appeal, held that a judge (one of some 129 temporary sheriffs) who had no security of tenure and whose appointment was subject to annual renewal was not 'independent' within the meaning of art 6 of the Convention. Lord Reed stated that the Scots system created a situation in which the temporary sheriff was liable to have hopes and fears in respect of his treatment by the Executive when his appointment came up for renewal: in short, a relationship of dependency. He described security of tenure as a cornerstone of judicial independence, and held that the prosecution of a trial before a temporary sheriff was incompetent under s 57(2) of the Scotland Act 1998.

1 1999 SCCR 1052.

1.68 In *Clancy v Caird*[1], the Inner House of the Court of Session distinguished *Starrs* and held that art 6 was not violated where a temporary judge heard and determined a civil dispute between private parties which neither involved the

Crown nor raised questions of public importance. The court noted that, by contrast with temporary sheriffs, such temporary judges were appointed for longer periods and were not subject to removal during those periods.

1   2000 SLT 546.

1.69   As a result of the landmark judgment in *Starrs*, the system of temporary sheriffs has been abolished, and reforms have been made in England and Wales and Northern Ireland. On 12 April 2000, the Lord Chancellor announced[1] that he, the Lord Chief Justice of England and Wales, and the Lord Chief Justice of Northern Ireland had agreed new arrangements for part-time judicial appointments, for which the Lord Chancellor was to be responsible, to underpin their independence. The changes came into effect immediately. Part-time appointments will be for a period of no fewer than five years, subject to the relevant upper age limit. There are five grounds for removal from office:

(1) misbehaviour;
(2) incapacity;
(3) persistent failure to comply with sitting requirements, without good reason;
(4) failure to comply with training requirements; and
(5) sustained failure to observe the standards reasonably expected from a holder of such an office.

The Lord Chief Justice will have to concur with any decision to remove which the Lord Chancellor proposes to take, following an investigation by a Judge nominated by the Lord Chief Justice. Where appointments are renewable, five-year renewals will generally be automatic. In addition to the five grounds for removal, there are two further grounds for non-renewal:

(1) part of a reduction in numbers because of changes in operational requirements; and
(2) part of a structural change to enable recruitment of new appointees.

Decisions not to renew will be decided on a 'first in, first out' basis by the Lord Chancellor with the concurrence of the Lord Chief Justice. The Lord Chancellor has also decided that no useful purpose is served by retaining the separate offices of Assistant Recorder and Recorder. All serving Assistant Recorders have therefore been appointed Recorders, and in future, appointments will be made direct to Recordership through an open, advertised selection procedure.

1   612 HL Official Report (5th series), WA42 (12 April 2000); New Law Journal, 21 April 2000, at 568.

1.70   The Lord Chancellor has also established an independent review of tribunals, chaired by Sir Andrew Leggatt, with one of its terms of reference being to ensure that the 'administrative and practical arrangements' for supporting tribunal decision-making procedures 'meet the requirements of the European Convention on Human Rights for independence and impartiality'[1]. This review is to be concluded by March 2001.

1   613 HL Official Report (5th series) (18 May 2000), WA 31. See further, http://www.tribunals-review.org.uk/.

1.71   In *Smith v Secretary of State for Trade and Industry*[1], Mr Justice Morison, President of the Employment Appeal Tribunal stated that 'there was a real and troubling question as to whether employment tribunals may properly and lawfully adjudicate on claims made against the Secretary of State, having regard to art 6 of the Convention', which gives everyone the right to have his civil rights determined by an 'independent and impartial' tribunal. There is an appearance of a lack of impartiality of employment tribunals when adjudicating on such claims because their lay members are appointed by the Secretary of State and are paid by him, their appointment may be terminated by the Secretary of State, the rules of procedure for tribunals are made by the Secretary of State, and the Department for Trade and Industry provides funds to the employment tribunal service. The appellant was given leave to appeal against the order remitting his case to an employment tribunal so as to give him the opportunity to argue that, having regard to the Convention, an employment tribunal could not adjudicate upon his complaint. However, an appeal was not pursued. In response to a Parliamentary Question tabled by Lord Lester of Herne Hill QC, Lord Sainsbury of Turville, Minister for Science, Department of Trade and Industry, said that the Government 's opinion was that 'employment tribunals may properly and lawfully adjudicate in such cases. Nevertheless, following the Lord Chancellor's review of the terms of service of part-time judicial office holders, we are reviewing the employment tribunal system and expect to make some changes to the terms and conditions of lay members'[2].

1   [2000] ICR 69, [2000] IRLR 6, EAT.
2   613 HL Official Report (5th series) (17 May 2000), WA 25.

1.72   In *Hoekstra v HM Advocate (No 2)*[1], the High Court of Justiciary held that the tone of an article published by a judge, Lord McCluskey, in a major newspaper gave the impression of deep seated hostility to the ECHR. This was enough in the circumstances to have created in the mind of an informed observer a sufficient apprehension of bias on the part of Lord McCluskey for the decision in question to be set aside.

1   2000 SCCR 367.

1.73   In *R v Secretary of State for the Home Department, ex p Simms*, the House of Lords held that where a fundamental or basic right is at stake (such as the right to free expression), even in the absence of an ambiguity, subordinate and primary legislation must be construed in accordance with the constitutional principle of legality. Parliament must, in Lord Hoffmann's words (at 341f–g)

'squarely confront what it is doing and accept the political cost. Fundamental rights cannot be overridden by general or ambiguous words. This is because there is too great a risk that the full implications of their unqualified meaning may have passed unnoticed in the democratic process. In the absence of express language or necessary implication to the contrary, the courts therefore presume that even the most general words were intended to be subject to the basic rights of the individual. In this way the courts of the United Kingdom, though acknowledging the sovereignty of Parliament, apply principles of constitutionality little different from those which exist in countries where the power of the legislature is expressly limited by a constitutional document'[2].

1   [1999] 3 WLR 328.
2   See also Lord Steyn (at 340f–g) with whose speech the other Law Lords concurred; and *B (a Minor) v DPP* [2000] 2 WLR 452 HL, at 463H–64D, *per* Lord Steyn. See also para **2.3.2** below.

1.74   In *R v Lord Saville of Newdigate, ex p A*[1], the Court of Appeal held that a decision maker was not entitled to reach a decision that risked interfering with fundamental rights in the absence of a compelling justification, and accordingly where such rights were engaged, the range of options open to a reasonable decision-maker was curtailed. In such a case, the court would anxiously scrutinise the strength of the countervailing circumstances and the degree of interference with the human right involved. The more substantial the interference, the more the court would require by way of justification before it was satisfied that the decision was reasonable[2]. In the particular case, the tribunal had failed to attach sufficient significance to the risk posed to the safety of former soldiers and their families, a risk which concerned the most fundamental right of all namely, the right to life.

1   [1999] 4 All ER 860.
2   See para **2.03,** n 6.

1.75   In *R v Lord Chancellor, ex p Lightfoot*[1], where a mandatory deposit was required under the Insolvency Fees Order 1986, as security for the fee to be paid to the Official Receiver for the performance of his duties on the making of a bankruptcy order, the Court of Appeal held that the requirement was not for access to the court but towards the costs of services provided by others for the benefit of the petitioning debtor, that the debtor did not have a constitutional right to be rehabilitated under the scheme, and that the debtor's Convention rights under arts 6 and 14 had not been violated.

1   [2000] 2 WLR 318.

1.76   In *R v North and East Devon Health Authority, ex p Coughlan*, where a severely disabled individual was moved from hospital to a purpose-built National Health Service facility upon a promise by the health authority that the facility would be her home for life, the Court of Appeal decided that the trial judge had been entitled to find that the authority had abused its powers not only by acting in breach of her legitimate expectation of a benefit, but also by acting in breach of her right to respect for her home, guaranteed by art 8.

1   [2000] 2 WLR 622.

1.77   In *R v Secretary of State for Health, ex p Eastside Cheese Co*[1], where cheese had been seized under an emergency control order, the Court of Appeal held that the interference with the respondents' right to the peaceful enjoyment of their possession, guaranteed by Article 1 of the First Protocol to the Convention, came within the exception for the control of property and was proportionate to the legitimate aim of responding to what the Secretary of State reasonably regarded as an imminent risk to the life or health of the public (from the E-coli 0157 bacteria), even though no compensation was payable for the resulting loss to the respondents' business.

1   [1999] Eu LR 968.

1.78   In *Woolgar v Chief Constable of Sussex Police*[1], the Court of Appeal held the public interest in maintaining the confidentiality of information disclosed to the police in criminal investigations had to be balanced against a countervailing public interest in protecting public health and safety, which entitled the police to disclose confidential information to a regulatory body which was reasonably believed to be relevant to an inquiry being conducted by that body. Kennedy LJ considered there was no breach of art 8 because the interest in public safety and health justified the breach of confidentiality in this case.

1   [2000] 1 WLR 25.

1.79   In *Reynolds v Times Newspapers Ltd*[1], the House of Lords refused to develop the common law of defamation by recognising a new category of qualified privilege for the publication by the media of political information. However, it did recognise that qualified privilege would be available for the publication of political information and other matters of serious public concern where the circumstances created a duty by the media to publish the information to the public. Lord Nicholls of Birkenhead, who gave the leading speech, observed (at 1023a–c) that freedom of expression will be buttressed by HRA 1988 s 12 (see para **2.12**), and that, when the HRA 1998 is fully in force, the common law must be developed and applied in a manner consistent with art 10.

> 'The interest of a democratic society in ensuring a free press weighs heavily in the balance in deciding whether any curtailment of this freedom bears a reasonable relationship to the purpose of the curtailment. In this regard it should be kept in mind that one of the contemporary functions of the media is investigative journalism. This activity, as much as the traditional activities of reporting and commenting, is part of the vital role of the press and the media generally'.

Lord Steyn observed (at 1029g–30c) that there is a basic and fundamental constitutional right to freedom of expression. When the HRA 1998 is fully in force, the constitutional dimension of freedom of expression will be reinforced. The starting point is the right to freedom of expression:

> 'a right based on a constitutional or higher legal order foundation. Exceptions to freedom of expression must be justified as being necessary in a democracy. In other words, freedom of expression is the rule and regulation of speech is the exception requiring justification. The existence and width of any exception can only be justified if it is underpinned by a pressing social need'.

Lord Steyn also recognised (at 1036c–h), relying upon Convention case law, that the press has a general duty to inform the public on political and other matters of public interest.

1   [1999] 3 WLR 1010.

1.80   In *R v Secretary of State for Health, ex p Wagstaff*[1], Kennedy LJ restated the principle that freedom of expression was recognised in the common law as a fundamental right even before the coming into effect of the HRA. The Divisional Court emphasised the importance of this fundamental right in holding that the decision of the Secretary of State to direct that the inquiry into the Dr Harold Shipman affair take place in private was irrational[2].

1   (20 July 2000, unreported).
2   See further para **4.10.6**.

1.81   In *R v Central Criminal Court, ex p The Guardian*[1], the Divisional Court allowed in part an appeal against orders requiring newspapers and journalists to disclose material relating to contacts that had been made with the ex-M16 agent,

Mr David Shayler. The Court interpreted Schedule 1, para 2(c) of the Police and Criminal Evidence Act 1984 as permitting a judge to take into account matters relevant to the public interest, in particular fundamental principles, in deciding whether to grant an order for disclosure. Judge LJ explained that these principles included the right to free speech and the necessary to maintain the independence and impartiality of the press. He regarded these principles as 'red in the bone' of the common law, and 'encapsulated and reflected' in the ECHR case law. Judge LJ then cited the speech of Lord Steyn in *Simms* (see para **1.73**) in serving that compelling evidence would normally be needed to demonstrate that the public interest is served by the seizure of such evidence[2].

1   (21 July 2000, unreported).
2   See further para **4.10.12B**.

1.82   In *Brown v Chief Constable of Avon and Somerest Constabulary*[1] the Divisional Court (Lord Bingham LCJ and Astill J) held that whereas s 2 of the Crime and Disorder Act 1998 did not expressly enact what standard of proof was to be applied on an application for a sex offender order, the clear intention of Parliament was that the civil standard of proof was appropriate. Lord Bingham LCJ rejected the contention that the proceedings would be regarded as criminal for the purposes of the ECHR, while recognising that the E Ct HR, in deciding whether there is a criminal charge for the purposes of art 6, has regard to the classification of proceedings in domestic law, but also to the nature of the offence itself and the severity of the potential penalties. Given the absence of any penalty arising from the imposition of the order itself, there was no requirement under the Convention that this procedure should attract the criminal standard of proof.

1   (26 April 2000, unreported).

1.83   In *R v Perry*[1], Swinton Thomas LJ held that a reference to art 8 of the ECHR in a challenge to the admission of identification evidence obtained in clear breach of the PACE Codes of Practice was inappropriate. The appeal could be disposed of under domestic law alone, and the Convention could be brought into disrepute by excessive and inappropriate references in such identification cases. In the judge's opinion, 'The Convention had been promulgated following the horrors of the Second World War and had been intended to protect citizens from true abuses of human rights but now it appeared that lawyers were jumping on the bandwagon. In that context it was possible not only that the appeals of others might be unjustly delayed but also that the Convention and the 1998 Act might themselves be brought into disrepute'.

1   (2000) Times, 28 April, CA.

1.84   A similar warning against the irresponsible citation of Convention arguments and cases was given by Lord Woolf MR for the Court of Appeal in *Daniels v Walker*[1]: 'if the court is not going to be taken down blind alleys it is essential that counsel, and those who instructed counsel, take a responsible attitude as to when it is right to raise a HRA point'[2].

1   [2000] 1 WLR 1382.
2   See similarly *North West Lancashire Health Authority v A, D and G* [2000] 1 WLR 977 (Court of Appeal), at 995D (Auld LJ), 1003A–C (Buxton LJ), 1003G–H (May LJ). See also para **2.2** below.

Chapter 2
Human Rights Act 1998

2.01 [*Contd*] On the general impact of the HRA 1998, note that in *R v DPP, ex p Kebilene*[2], Lord Hope of Craighead observed:

'It is now plain that the incorporation of the European Convention on Human Rights into our domestic law will subject the entire system to a fundamental process of review and, where necessary, reform by the judiciary'.

See also *Starrs v Ruxton*[3], per Lord Reid :

'The effect given to the European Convention by the Scotland Act and the Human Rights Act in particular represents, to my mind, a very important shift in thinking about the constitution. It is fundamental to that shift that human rights are no longer dependent solely on conventions, by which I mean values, customs and practices of the constitution which are not legally enforceable. Although the Convention protects rights which reflect democratic values and underpin democratic institutions, the Convention guarantees the protection of those rights through legal processes, rather than political processes'.

2   [1999] 3 WLR 972, 988E.
3   1999 SCCR 1052 (High Court of Justiciary).

2.2 [*Contd*] See *Starrs v Ruxton*[3] per Lord Reid, in applying the 1998 Act:

'the starting point for any consideration of the European Convention must be the Strasbourg jurisprudence : any other material lacks its authority and can only be of persuasive value. I also accept that it is essential to treat with caution decisions concerned with other constitutional instruments. It may be tempting to look for assistance, in the interpretation and application of the Convention, to decisions emanating from legal systems belonging to the same tradition as our own; but it is important to remember that the Convention jurisprudence has been influenced principally by the traditions of other European legal systems, and that decisions from common law jurisdictions may therefore be misleading. Nevertheless, the Canadian Charter of Rights and Freedoms is similar in some respects to the European Convention, and the Canadian courts have had regard to the Strasbourg jurisprudence in their interpretation of the Charter. In these circumstances, their decisions are potentially a useful source, albeit one which has to be treated with care'.

See similarly *Williams v Cowell*[4] per Mummery LJ for the Court of Appeal:

'when human rights points are taken there is a temptation to impress (and oppress) the court with bulk and to turn a judicial hearing of a particular case into an international human rights seminar. This temptation should be resisted. There should only be put before the court that part of the researched material which is reasonably required for the resolution of the particular appeal. It is not necessary to include all the treaty, convention, legislative, judicial and periodical material which has been uncovered'.

See also paras **1.81–1.82** above.

3   1999 SCCR 1052 (High Court of Justiciary).
4   [2000] 1 WLR 187, 198D–E.

2.3.2 [*Contd*] In *R v Secretary of State for the Home Department, ex p Simms*[3], Lord Steyn (for the Appellate Committee of the House of Lords) explained at 340F–H that under the law prior to the HRA 1998, there existed a 'principle of legality' under which there is a presumption 'even in the absence of an ambiguity' that the law is consistent with fundamental constitutional principles, such as access to justice. Lord Hoffmann added, at 341F–342C, that 'fundamental rights cannot be overridden by general or ambiguous words' and

> 'The Human Rights Act 1998 will make three changes to this scheme of things. First, the principles of fundamental human rights which exist at common law will be supplemented by a specific text, namely the European Convention on Human Rights and Fundamental Freedoms. But much of the Convention reflects the common law : see *Derbyshire County Council v Times Newspapers Ltd* [1993] AC 534, 551. That is why the United Kingdom government felt able in 1950 to accede to the Convention without domestic legislative change. So the adoption of the text as part of domestic law is unlikely to involve radical change in our notions of fundamental human rights. Secondly, the principle of legality will be expressly enacted as a rule of construction in section 3 and will gain further support from the obligation of the Minister in charge of a Bill to make a statement of compatibility under section 19. Thirdly, in those unusual cases in which the legislative infringement of fundamental human rights is so clearly expressed as not to yield to the principle of legality, the courts will be able to draw this to the attention of Parliament by making a declaration of incompatibility. It will then be for the sovereign Parliament to decide whether or not to remove the incompatibility'.

On the principle of legality, see also Lord Steyn in *B (A Minor) v DPP*[4]. See also para **1.73** above.

In *R v DPP, ex p Kebilene*[5], Lord Cooke of Thorndon commented that s 3 of the 1998 Act contains 'a strong adjuration' and is a 'powerful message' to the court.

3   [1999] 3 WLR 328.
4   [2000] 2 WLR 452, 463G–464C.
5   [1999] 3 WLR 972, 987C and F.

2.3.5 [*Contd*] In *R v DPP, ex p Kebilene*[1], Lord Steyn commented:

> 'It is crystal clear that the carefully and subtly drafted Human Rights Act 1998 preserves the principle of Parliamentary sovereignty. In a case of incompatibility, which cannot be avoided by interpretation under section 3(1), the courts may not disapply the legislation. The court may merely issue a declaration of incompatibility which then gives rise to a power to take remedial action: see section 10'.

1   [1999] 3 WLR 972, 981D.

2.6.2 [*Contd*] See *Starrs v Ruxton*[5], per the Lord Justice Clerk, Lord Cullen: s 6(2)

> 'is plainly intended to refer to an act of the public authority which is required by primary legislation'.

5   1999 SCCR 1052 (High Court of Justiciary).

2.6.3

2   [*Contd*] On the meaning of a public authority, see the guidance discussed at para **1.54** above.
3   [*Contd*] On the application of the HRA to litigation between private parties, see Sir Richard Buxton *The Human Rights Act and Private Law* (2000) 116 LQR 48, Professor HWR Wade *Horizons of Horizontality* (2000) 116 LQR 217, and a reply by Lord Lester of Herne Hill QC and David Pannick QC

The Impact of the Human Rights Act on Private Law: The Knight's Move (2000) 116 LQR 380 and Jack Beatson and Stephen Grosz *Horizontalilty: A Footnote* (2000) LQR 385.

2.7.1 [*Contd*] In *R v DPP, ex p Kebilene*[7], Lord Steyn commented that:

'it is rightly conceded that once the Act of 1998 is fully in force it will not be possible to apply for judicial review on the ground that a decision to prosecute is in breach of a Convention right. The only available remedies will be in the trial process or on appeal'.

That is because judicial review lies only where there is no alternative remedy[8].

7   [1999] 3 WLR 972, 984A.
8   See also Lord Hope of Craighead at 988H–989A.

2.7.2 [*Contd*] On section 7 and standing, see Karen Steyn and David Wolfe 'Judicial Review and the Human Rights Act: Some Practical Considerations'[18].

18   [1999] EHRLR 614.

2.13.1

2   [*Contd*] On the meaning of a 'religion' see also para **4.9.7** below.

2.19.1 [*Contd*] On s 19 statements, see paras **1.46–1.50** above.

2.22.3 In *R v DPP, ex p Kebilene*[3], Lord Steyn rejected the argument that s 22(4), read with s 7(1)(b), 'is apt only to extend to the trial. It was an argument of some technicality. The language of the statute does not compel its adoption and a construction which treats the trial and the appeal as parts of one process is more in keeping with the purpose of the Convention and the Act of 1998'. But see also Lord Hobhouse at Woodborough who pointed out, at 1008G that ss 3, 6 and 7 are not given retrospective effect.

3   [1999] 3 WLR 972, 982B–D.

2.22.4

2   [*Contd*] On the Isle and Man and the Channel Islands, see paras **1.60–1.62** above.

Chapter 3

Principles of interpretation

3.07 On pluralism and democracy as core values of the Convention, see *United Communist Party of Turkey v Turkey*[1].

1   (1998) 26 EHRR 121, 147-148, E Ct HR, paras 43–45.

3.10 On the principle of proportionality under EC law see *R v Secretary of State for Health, ex p Eastside Cheese Co (A Firm)*[1].

1   [1999] Eu LR 968 (Court of Appeal).

3.13 In *Hashman and Harrup v United Kingdom*[1], the E Ct HR held that the power of magistrates to bind-over a person to be of good behaviour was not prescribed by law, as required by art 10, because it failed to satisfy the principles stated at para 31 of the Judgment:

> 'A norm cannot be regarded a "law" unless it is formulated with sufficient precision to enable the citizen to regulate his conduct. At the same time, whilst uncertainty in the law is highly desirable, it may bring in its train excessive rigidity and the law must be able to keep pace with changing circumstances. The level of precision required of domestic legislation - which cannot in any case provide for every eventuality - depends to a considerable degree on the content of the instrument in question, the field it is designed to cover and the number and status of those to whom it is addressed ...'.

1   [2000] Crim LR 185, E Ct HR.

3.16 In *Lustig-Prean v United Kingdom*[1] (the policy of excluding homosexuals from the armed forces breached the right to private life), the E Ct HR said at paras 82–83 that the case concerned 'a most intimate aspect of an individuals's private life' in respect of which 'there must exist particularly serious reasons' before interferences on the part of the public authorities could be legitimate.

1   (1999) 29 EHRR 548, 580–581.

3.17 On Art 17 see Jonathan Cooper and Adrian Marshall Williams 'Hate Speech, Holocaust Denial and International Human Rights Law'[1].

1   [1999] EHRLR 593, 605–607.

3.20 *[Contd]* In *R v DPP, ex p Kebilene*[6], Lord Hope of Craighead expressly approved the suggestion in the text that although the doctrine of the margin of appreciation does not apply when national courts consider the application of the Human Rights Act 1998, courts will recognise a discretionary area of judgment for the legislature and executive on policy issues, with the intensity of scrutiny depending on the issues.

6   [1999] 3 WLR 972, 993F–994E.

4.2
Article 2 Right to life

4.2.1 [*Contd*] The E Ct HR continues to rank art 2 as 'one of the most fundamental provisions in the Convention' and has repeatedly stated that art 2, together with art 3, 'enshrines one of the basic values of the democratic societies making up the Council of Europe'[5]. The UK courts have similarly ranked an individual's right to life as 'the most fundamental of all human rights'[6], such that when the right to life is engaged, the options available to the reasonable decision-maker are curtailed[7].

5 *Ertak v Turkey* (9 May 2000, unreported), E Ct HR, para 134 and *Çakici v Turkey* (8 July 1999, unreported), E Ct HR, para 86.
6 *Bugdaycay v Secretary of State for the Home Department* [1987] AC 514 at 531E, *per* Lord Bridge of Harwich, cited with approval in *R v Lord Saville of Newdigate, ex p A* [1999] 4 All ER 860, CA concerning the risk to life posed by the withdrawal of anonymity from the soldiers appearing before the Saville Inquiry into Bloody Sunday.
7 See *R v Lord Saville of Newdigate, ex p A* [1999] 4 All ER 860 at paras 34–37, relying on *R v Ministry of Defence, ex p Smith* [1996] QB 517, CA.

4.2.4 [*Contd*] In keeping with the importance of art 2(2) in a democratic society, the E Ct HR must, in making its assessment, subject deprivations of life to the most careful scrutiny, particularly where deliberate force is used. However, the E Ct HR continues to reiterate that art 2(2) is not confined to cases of intentional killing[4]. Further guidance on what is an excessive use of force may be forthcoming as the E Ct HR has recently declared admissible four applications concerning the 'shoot to kill' policy of the Government in Northern Ireland[5].

4 *Ogur v Turkey* (20 May 1999, unreported), E Ct HR, para. 78.
5 'Admissibility decision in four cases against the United Kingdom', a press release issued by the Registrar, dated 5 April 2000. The four cases are *Jordan v United Kingdom, McKerr v United Kingdom, Kelly v United Kingdom* and *Shanaghan v United Kingdom.*

4.2.5 [*Contd*] Brothers and sisters may also bring complaints under art 2 concerning the death of their siblings[5]. Surviving parents and siblings, as well as surviving spouses[6] and children, may also be awarded non-pecuniary damages as regards the deceased where it is found that there had been arbitrary detention or torture before the deceased's disappearance or death[7].

5 *See Çakici v Turkey* (8 July 1999, unreported), E Ct HR (claim brought by brother of disappeared person), *Kiliç v Turkey* (28 March 2000, unreported), E Ct HR (claim brought by brother of murdered journalist) and *Mahmut Kaya v Turkey* (28 March 2000, unreported), E Ct HR (claim brought by brother of murdered doctor). *Yasa v Turkey* is now reported in (1999) 28 EHRR 408, E Ct HR.
6 Including *de facto* spouses: *Velikova v Bulgaria* (18 May 2000, unreported) E Ct HR.
7 *Kiliç v Turkey* (28 March 2000, unreported), E Ct HR, para 105 and *Mahmut Kaya v Turkey* (28 March 2000, unreported), E Ct HR, para 138, but note the dissent on this point entered by Judge Gölcüklü in both cases. However, in *Ertak v Turkey* (9 May 2000, unreported), E Ct HR, para 151, there is no dissent by Judge Gölcüklü.

4.2.6 [*Contd*] The E Ct HR continues to recall that the first sentence of art 2(1) enjoins the State not only to refrain from the intentional and unlawful taking of life, but also to take appropriate steps to safeguard the lives of those within its jurisdiction[2]. A State is therefore obliged by art 2 to put in place effective criminal law provisions to deter the commission of offences against the person backed up by law enforcement machinery for the prevention, suppression and punishment of breaches of such provisions[3]. It may also, in appropriate circumstances, be under a positive obligation to take preventive operational measures to protect an individual or individuals whose life is at risk from the criminal acts of another individual[4]. However, the scope of this positive obligation must be interpreted in a way which does not impose an impossible or disproportionate burden on the authorities, 'bearing in mind the difficulties in policing modern societies, the unpredictability of human conduct and the operational choices which must be made in terms of priorities and resources'[5].

2   *Kiliç v Turkey* (28 March 2000, unreported), E Ct HR, para 62 and *Mahmut Kaya v Turkey* (28 March 2000, unreported), E Ct HR, para 85, citing *LCB v United Kingdom* (1998) 27 EHRR 212, E Ct HR, para 36.
3   *Kiliç v Turkey* (28 March 2000, unreported), E Ct HR, para 62 and *Mahmut Kaya v Turkey* (28 March 2000, unreported), E Ct HR, para 85, citing *Osman v United Kingdom*, now reported in (1998) 29 EHRR 245, E Ct HR, para 115.
4   *Kiliç v Turkey* (28 March 2000, unreported), E Ct HR, para 62 and *Mahmut Kaya v Turkey* (28 March 2000, unreported), E Ct HR, para 85, citing *Osman v United Kingdom* (1998) 29 EHRR 245, E Ct HR, para 115.
5   *Kiliç v Turkey* (28 March 2000, unreported), E Ct HR, para 63 and *Mahmut Kaya v Turkey* (28 March 2000, unreported), E Ct HR, para 86. See also *Osman v United Kingdom* (1998) 29 EHRR 245, E Ct HR, para 116.

4.2.7   [*Contd*] Not every claimed risk to life can entail for the authorities a Convention requirement to take operational measures to prevent that risk from materialising. As established in *Osman v United Kingdom*[4], and successfully invoked in *Kiliç v Turkey*[5] and *Mahmut Kaya v Turkey*[6], for a violation of the positive obligation to protect the right to life to arise, 'it must be established that the authorities knew or ought to have known at the time of the existence of a real and immediate risk to the life of an identified individual or individuals from the criminal acts of a third party and that they failed to take measures within the scope of their powers which, judged reasonably, might have been expected to avoid that risk.' This is essentially a two-limb test with the first limb resting on the extent of the State's knowledge and the second limb resting on the reasonableness of the steps taken. As for the risk, it can be considered 'real and immediate' when the authorities are aware of a significant number of incidents involving the killing of persons similar to the individual concerned, who appear to have been targeted because of their political views by either the security forces or other non-State actors acting with the State's knowledge and acquiescence[7]. A request to the authorities for protective measures may also support a finding of a 'real and immediate' risk[8].

4   (1998) 29 EHRR 245, E Ct HR, para 116.
5   (28 March 2000, unreported), E Ct HR, para 64.
6   (28 March 2000, unreported), E Ct HR, para 87.
7   *Kiliç v Turkey* (28 March 2000, unreported), E Ct HR, para 66 and *Mahmut Kaya v Turkey* (28 March 2000, unreported), E Ct HR, paras 89–91. See also *Akkoç v Turkey* Application 22947–8/93 (23 April 1999, unreported), EComHR, para 274, currently pending before the E Ct HR.
8   *Kiliç v Turkey* (28 March 2000, unreported), E Ct HR, para 67. A request is not, however, decisive since none was made in *Mahmut Kaya v Turkey* (28 March 2000, unreported), E Ct HR.

4.2.8   [*Contd*] Certain defects may undermine the effectiveness of the criminal law provisions put in place by the State to protect the right to life. In both *Kiliç v*

Turkey[4] and *Mahmut Kaya v Turkey*[5], the E Ct HR held that defects which permitted or fostered a lack of accountability of the security forces for their actions undermined the legal protection accorded by the State to the right to life. These defects included the lack of an independent and effective procedure for investigating deaths involving members of the security forces, the repeated failure of the public prosecutors to pursue complaints by individuals claiming that the security forces were involved in an unlawful act, and the use of State Security Courts which did not comply with the requirement of independence imposed by art 6(1)[6].

4   (28 March 2000, unreported), E Ct HR, para 75.
5   (28 March 2000, unreported), E Ct HR, para 98.
6   *Kiliç v Turkey* (28 March 2000, unreported), E Ct HR, paras 71–75 and *Mahmut Kaya v Turkey* (28 March 2000, unreported), E Ct HR, paras 94–97.

4.2.9   [*Contd*] The absence of any operational measures of protection will also undermine the effectiveness of the protection accorded by a State to the right to life. Where there is no evidence of the authorities taking any steps in response to a request for protection, either by applying reasonable measures of protection or by investigating the extent of the alleged risk with a view to instituting any appropriate measures of prevention, the E Ct HR will likely conclude that the authorities have failed to take reasonable measures available to them to prevent a real and immediate risk to life[4].

4   *Kiliç v Turkey* (28 March 2000, unreported), E Ct HR, para 76. See also *Mahmut Kaya v Turkey* (28 March 2000, unreported), E Ct HR, paras 100–101.

4.2.10   [*Contd*] Notwithstanding its traditional reluctance in finding violations of the positive obligation to protect the right to life, the E Ct HR on 28 March 2000 held in two cases, by six votes to one, that Turkey had failed to protect two of its citizens from a known risk to their right to life[2]. There had, however, been a pattern of 'unknown perpetrator' killings in south-east Turkey at the time, which were allegedly committed by elements within the security forces, or contra-guerrilla groups acting under their *aegis*, thereby putting into question the rule of law in the region.

2   See *Kiliç v Turkey* (28 *March* 2000, unreported), E Ct HR and *Mahmut Kaya v Turkey* (28 March 2000, unreported), E Ct HR.

4.2.11   [*Contd*] Article 2 has generally been applied to cases where a person has been deprived of his or her life. However, in cases of serious injury, both the Court and Commission have considered complaints within the ambit of art 2 where the applicant has been subjected to a life-threatening attack but survived[5]. Such injuries may bring the complaint within the scope of the State's positive obligation to protect the right to life and where the injured person remains within the custody of the State authorities, a delay in obtaining appropriate medical treatment may disclose a failure to respect the right to life[6].

5   See *Osman v United Kingdom* (1998) 29 EHRR 245, E Ct HR (child applicant shot during attack in which father died); *Yasa v Turkey* (1999) 28 EHRR 408, E Ct HR (applicant hit by eight bullets during attempt on life); and *Ilhan v Turkey* (23 April 1999, unreported) EComHR (applicant's brother partially paralysed from life-threatening blow to head).
6   See *Ilhan v Turkey* 22277/93 (23 April 1999, unreported), EComHR, paras 220–221. The E Ct HR, however, considered the delay within the ambit of art 3: *Ilhan v Turkey* (27 June 2000, unreported), E Ct HR.

4.2.17 [*Contd*] In a recent decision of the South Africa High Court, Transvaal Provincial Division concerning an attempt to expand 'everyone' to include the unborn child, McCrath J held that while at common law the status of a foetus was uncertain, it was clear that in comparable jurisdictions, such as England, the US and Canada, a foetus only gained rights if it was subsequently born alive[1].

1   *Christian Lawyers Association of South Africa v Minister of Health* (1998) 50 BMLR 241.

4.2.24 [*Contd*] The United Kingdom has further confirmed its position in favour of the abolition of the death penalty. On 10 December 1999, the United Kingdom[3] ratified the Second Optional Protocol[4] to the *International Covenant on Civil and Political Rights* which is aimed at the universal abolition of the death penalty. The Protocol entered into force for the United Kingdom on 10 March 2000. Article 1(1) provides that 'No one within the jurisdiction of a State Party to the present Protocol shall be executed,' without any limitation with respect to peacetime, while art 1(2) provides that 'Each State Party shall take all necessary measures to abolish the death penalty within its jurisdiction.'

3   Also in respect of the Bailiwick of Guernsey, the Bailiwick of Jersey and the Isle of Man.
4   Cm 4676 (April 2000). For the text of the Second Optional Protocol, see Appendix 2, pp 430–31.

4.2.26 [*Contd*] In *Aspichi Dehwari v Netherlands*, a claim was brought by an Iranian dissident alleging that his proposed expulsion to Iran would expose him to a serious risk of being killed, either extra-judicially or following an unfair trial on trumped up charges leading to the death penalty. On the facts, the Commission found no violation of art 2, although its reasoning did not exclude the possibility that an issue might arise under art 2 or art 1 of the Sixth Protocol in circumstances in which the expelling State knowingly puts the person concerned at such a high risk of losing his life as for the outcome to be a near-certainty[3]. The Commission, however, went on to suggest that such a risk was more likely to place the expulsion within the ambit of art 3 rather than art 2[4]. The case was then referred to the E Ct HR. In January 2000, the applicant withdrew his complaint upon receiving a residence permit from the Netherlands. In its decision to strike the case off the list[5], the E Ct HR reiterated the test it established in *Soering v United Kingdom*[6], placing the case, by implication, firmly within the ambit of art 3 rather than art 2 and the Sixth Protocol[7].

3   *Aspichi Dehwari v Netherlands* (29 October 1998, unreported) EComHR, para 61. See *also X v Netherlands* (9 July 1998, unreported), EComHR, paras 56–57.
4   *Aspichi Dehwari v Netherlands* (29 October 1998, unreported), EComHR, para 61.
5   *Aspichi Dehwari v Netherlands* (27 April 2000, unreported), E Ct HR, para 17.
6   (1989) 11 EHRR 439, E Ct HR, paras 90–91.
7   See also *Abdurrahim Incedursun v Netherlands* (22 June 1999, unreported), E Ct HR, striking off a similar case involving a proposed expulsion to Turkey, although the Sixth Protocol claim was less cogent given the Turkish moratorium on the death penalty.

4.2.27 [*Contd*] The reasons given by the E Ct HR in its decision to strike out both *Aspichi Dehwari v Netherlands*[4] and *Abdurrahim Incedursun v Netherlands*[5] suggest that a real risk of extra-judicial killings upon expulsion is more likely to be considered under art 3 than art 2.

4   (27 April 2000, unreported), E Ct HR.
5   (22 June 1999, unreported), E Ct HR.

4.2.28 [*Contd*] The evidentiary standard for establishing that a State's security forces or police officers are implicated in an unlawful killing is proof beyond all reasonable doubt. The E Ct HR has, however, reiterated 'that while the attainment of the required evidentiary standard ... may follow from the co-existence of sufficiently strong, clear and concordant inferences or unrebutted presumptions, their evidential value must be assessed in the light of the circumstances of the individual case and the seriousness and nature of the charge to which they give rise against the respondent State'[5]. In certain circumstances, inferences may be drawn where a State without good reason fails to produce material requested of it[6].

5   *Tanrikulu v Turkey* (8 July 1999, unreported), E Ct HR, para 97, citing *Yasa v Turkey* (1999) 28 EHRR 408, E Ct HR, para 96.
6   *Tanrikulu v Turkey* (8 July 1999, unreported), E Ct HR, para 98.

4.2.30 [*Contd*] The Commission's decision in *Ogur v Turkey* as regards the planning and execution of an armed operation which led to the death of a night-watchman has since found favour with a Grand Chamber of the E Ct HR[7]. The Court's decision emphasises the need for the issuance of warnings in such cases, although on the facts, the Court found that even supposing that Ogur had been killed by a bullet fired as a warning, the firing of that shot was so badly executed as to constitute gross negligence, thereby attracting State responsibility under art 2[8].

2   See *Kaya v Turkey* (1998) 28 EHRR 1, E Ct HR; *Kurt v Turkey* (1999) 27 EHRR 373, E Ct HR; *Mentes v Turkey* (1997) 26 EHRR 595, E Ct HR; *Ergi v Turkey* 1998-IV RJD 1778, E Ct HR; *Güleç v Turkey* (1999) 28 EHRR 121, E Ct HR; and *Yasa v Turkey* (1999) 28 EHRR 408, E Ct HR.
4   On the use of plastic bullets or 'baton rounds', see Jason-Lloyd, 'Plastic Bullets on the Mainland' (1990) 140 NLJ 1492 and Robertson, 'Baton Rounds in Great Britain' (1991) 141 NLJ 340. See also *Stewart v United Kingdom* 39 DR 162 (1984), EComHR, concerning the death of the applicant's son after being hit on the head by a plastic bullet fired into a crowd of rioters. The UN Committee against Torture has expressed concern about the UK's use of plastic bullets as a means of riot control and recommended its abolition: UN Doc A/54/44.
5   *Güleç v Turkey* (1999) 28 EHRR 121, E Ct HR, para 71.
7   *Ogur v Turkey* (20 May 1999, unreported), E Ct HR.
8   *Ogur v Turkey* (20 May 1999, unreported), E Ct HR, paras 82–83.

4.2.32 [*Contd*] The E Ct HR continues to reiterate that the obligation to protect life under art 2, read in conjunction with the State's general duty under art 1, requires by implication that there should be some form of effective official investigation when individuals have been killed as a result of the use of force[5]. This obligation is not confined to cases where it has been established that the killing was caused by an agent of the State[6], and nor is it confined to cases of intentional killings[7]. It is also not relieved by the existence of a security situation in the State causing the frequent loss of life and hampering the search for conclusive evidence[8]. A Grand Chamber of seventeen judges has also confirmed the decisions of the seven-member Chambers in *Ergi v Turkey*[9] and *Yasa v Turkey*[10] that the mere fact that the authorities were informed of a death can give rise *ipso facto* to an obligation under art 2 to carry out an effective investigation into the circumstances surrounding the death[11].

3   1998-IV RJD 1778, E Ct HR.
5   See *Velikova v Bulgaria* (18 May 2000, unreported), E Ct HR, para 80; *Kiliç v Turkey* (28 March 2000, unreported), E Ct HR, para 78; *Mahmut Kaya v Turkey* (28 March 2000, unreported), E Ct HR, para 102; and *Tanrikulu v Turkey* (8 July 1999, unreported), E Ct HR, para 101, citing *McCann v*

United Kingdom (1996) 21 EHRR 97, E Ct HR, para 161 and *Kaya v Turkey*, now reported in (1999) 28 EHRR 1, E Ct HR, para 86. See also *Ertak v Turkey* (9 May 2000, unreported), E Ct HR, para 134 and *Ogur v Turkey* (20 May 1999, unreported), E Ct HR, para 88, citing *Yasa v Turkey* (1999) 28 EHRR 408, E Ct HR, para. 88.

6   *Tanrikulu v Turkey* (8 July 1999, unreported), E Ct HR, para 103. See also *Yasa v Turkey*, now reported in (1999) 28 EHRR 408, E Ct HR, para 100.

7   *Çakici v Turkey* (8 July 1999, unreported), E Ct HR, para 86.

8   *Tanrikulu v Turkey* (8 July 1999, unreported), E Ct HR, para 110.

9   1998-IV RJD 1778, E Ct HR, para 82.

10   (1999) 28 EHRR 408, E Ct HR, para 100.

11   *Tanrikulu v Turkey* (8 July 1999, unreported), E Ct HR, para 103.

4.2.33 [*Contd*] As in *Kaya v Turkey*[4], the E Ct HR in *Tanrikulu v Turkey*[5] could not conclude beyond reasonable doubt that the applicant's husband was killed by the security forces, or with their connivance, but nevertheless found a violation of art 2 as a result of the inadequacy of the investigation[6]. Similarly, in *Kiliç v Turkey*[7] and *Mahmut Kaya v Turkey*[8], it could not be established beyond reasonable doubt that the State was involved in the killing of a journalist and doctor respectively, but the E Ct HR nevertheless found a violation of art 2 on the grounds of an inadequate investigation, as well as a violation of the positive obligation to protect the right to life.

4   Now reported in (1999) 28 EHRR 1, E Ct HR.

5   (8 July 1999, unreported), E Ct HR.

6   See also *Önen v Turkey* (10 September 1999, unreported) EComHR.

7   (28 March 2000, unreported), E Ct HR.

8   (28 March 2000, unreported), E Ct HR.

4.2.34 [*Contd*] An 'effective official investigation' is one that is 'thorough, impartial and careful'[2]. It must also be capable of leading to the identification and punishment of those responsible for the killing[3]. With respect to the requirements for an adequate investigation, 'it is not possible to reduce the variety of situations which might occur to a bare check list of acts'[4]. It can however be noted that the E Ct HR has been critical of superficial investigations, inadequate and imprecise reporting at the various stages of an investigation, poorly conducted autopsies and inadequate forensic examinations, and the absence of statements from potential eyewitnesses[5]. The limited scope and short duration of an investigation may also ground a violation of the investigatory obligation under art 2[6], as will significant delays[7]. Where there are serious allegations of misconduct and infliction of harm implicating officers of the State, it is incumbent on the investigating authorities to 'respond actively and with reasonable expedition'[8]. An independent and public investigation is also required[9].

2   *Velikova v Bulgaria* (18 May 2000, unreported), E Ct HR, para 80.

3   *Ogur v Turkey* (20 May 1999, unreported), E Ct HR, para 88.

4   *Velikova v Bulgaria* (18 May 2000, unreported), E Ct HR, para 80.

5   See, for example, *Tanrikulu v Turkey* (8 July 1999, unreported), E Ct HR, paras 104–110 and *Ogur v Turkey* (20 May 1999, unreported), E Ct HR, paras 89–93.

6   *Kiliç v Turkey* (28 March 2000, unreported), E Ct HR, para 83.

7   *Mahmut Kaya v Turkey* (28 March 2000, unreported), E Ct HR, para 106.

8   *Mahmut Kaya v Turkey* (28 March 2000, unreported), E Ct HR, para 107.

9   *Ertak v Turkey* (9 May 2000, unreported), E Ct HR, para 134 and *Ogur v Turkey* (20 May 1999, unreported), E Ct HR, para 91.

4.2.34A   Finding a violation of art 2 on the ground that no effective investigation has been conducted into an unlawful death can also raise a separate issue under art 13, the requirements of which are broader that the obligation to investigate under art 2[1]. The E Ct HR has repeatedly held that a violation of the investigatory obligation under art 2 does not preclude a separate art 13 claim[2].

1 On art 13 generally, see paras **4.13.1–4.13.17**.
2 *Velikova v Bulgaria* (18 May 2000, unreported), E Ct HR, para 90; *Kiliç v Turkey* (28 March 2000, unreported), E Ct HR, para 93; *Mahmut Kaya v Turkey* (28 March 2000, unreported), E Ct HR, para 126; *Tanrikulu v Turkey* (8 July 1999, unreported), E Ct HR, paras 118–119; *Çakici v Turkey* (8 July 1999, unreported), E Ct HR, para 114; and *Kaya v Turkey* (1999) 28 EHRR 1, E Ct HR, para 107.

4.2.35 *[Contd]* The E Ct HR has now confirmed that 'where an individual is taken into police custody in good health but is later found dead, it is incumbent on the State to provide a plausible explanation of the events leading to his death, failing which the authorities must be held responsible under Article 2 of the Convention'[3]. In assessing the evidence, the E Ct HR applies the standard of proof of 'beyond reasonable doubt'[4] although such proof may follow from the co-existence of sufficiently strong, clear and concordant inferences, or similarly unrebutted presumptions of fact[5]. Moreover, where the events in issue lie wholly, or in large part, within the exclusive knowledge of the authorities, as in the cases of detainees, strong presumptions of fact will arise in respect of injuries and death occurring during that detention. The authorities will therefore be required to provide a satisfactory and convincing explanation. The existence of this obligation is not affected by the fact that the death or injury occurs as a result of the prisoner's attempts, successful or otherwise, to commit suicide, although its scope cannot extend to the imposition of a regime so rigorous that any attempt at self-injury would be impossible[6].

3 *Velikova v Bulgaria* (18 May 2000, unreported), E Ct HR, para 70 and *Salman v Turkey* (27 June 2000, unreported), E Ct HR, para 99, citing in support the art 3 decision of *Selmouni v France* (2000) 29 EHRR 403, E Ct HR, para 87.
4 *Ireland v UK* (1978) 2 EHRR 25, E Ct HR, para 61.
5 *Velikova v Bulgaria* (18 May 2000, unreported), E Ct HR, para 70.
6 *Keenan v United Kingdom* (6 September 1999, unreported), EComHR, para 79. In its decision on the merits, the majority in *Keenan* concluded that the prison authorities had done all that could be reasonably expected of them.

4.2.36 *[Contd]* The test for proving a 'disappearance' in violation of art 2 has been modified by the E Ct HR since its decision in *Kurt v Turkey*[6]. In *Çakici v Turkey*[7], a Grand Chamber of the E Ct HR found Turkey in violation of art 2 in respect of the presumed death of a Turkish citizen who had disappeared after being detained and tortured by the security forces. The detention and torture were unacknowledged by the Turkish authorities who took the view that Ahmet Çakici had been killed during an armed clash with the security forces, claiming that his identity card had been found on the body of a dead terrorist. There was, however, no evidence as to the identification of the body and nor was the body released for burial, leading the Commission and Court to draw 'very strong inferences' from the authorities' claim. On this basis, the E Ct HR held that there was 'sufficient circumstantial evidence, based on concrete elements, on which it may be concluded beyond reasonable doubt that Ahmet Çakici died following his apprehension and detention by the security forces'[8]. The E Ct HR also distinguished *Kurt v Turkey*, noting that in *Kurt*, no other elements of evidence existed concerning the detained individual's treatment or subsequent fate[9]. The Court further observed that no explanation had been provided by the authorities as to what had happened to Çakici after his apprehension by the *gendarmes* and nor was any justification relied upon in respect of any use of lethal force[10]. In May 2000, a seven-member Chamber of the E Ct HR distinguished *Kurt* on similar grounds in the disappearance case of *Ertak v Turkey*[11].

6   Now reported in (1999) 27 EHRR 373, E Ct HR.
7   (8 July 1999, unreported), E Ct HR.
8   *Çakici v Turkey* (8 July 1999, unreported), E Ct HR, para 85. A similar approach was taken in *Ertak v Turkey* (9 May 2000, unreported), E Ct HR, para. 131; *Tas v Turkey* (9 September 1999, unreported), EComHR, para 202; and *Akdeniz and Others v Turkey* (10 September 1999, unreported), EComHR, para 477.
9   *Çakici v Turkey* (8 July 1999, unreported), E Ct HR, para 85.
10   *Çakici v Turkey* (8 July 1999, unreported), E Ct HR, para 87.
11   (9 May 2000, unreported), E Ct HR, paras 131–132.

4.2.37   [*Contd*] In September 1999, a fourth application by Cyprus against Turkey relating to the consequences of the Turkish military operations in Northern Cyprus in 1974 was referred to the E Ct HR for examination[5]. In its report on the merits, now made public, the Commission found Turkey in violation of art 2 by virtue of the lack of an effective investigation with respect to the fate of the Greek Cypriots who had disappeared in Northern Cyprus[6]. In its view, these persons had disappeared in circumstances which were no doubt life-threatening since at the relevant time killings occurred on a large scale and in some cases, such killings were not the result of acts of war, but of criminal behaviour outside the fighting zone. Turkey was therefore under a continuing obligation to investigate in view of the fact that the Greek Cypriot missing persons might have lost their lives as a result of crimes[7]. The Commission also found that Turkey had not discharged this obligation with the help of an international investigatory body, namely the UN Committee on Missing Persons, since that body could not enquire into the causes for any deaths, nor establish any responsibilities[8]. The ability of the investigatory authority to conduct an independent investigation will also be important, as confirmed by the decision of the E Ct HR in *Ogur v Turkey*[9].

5   See 'Case of Cyprus against Turkey referred to the European Court of Human Rights', a press release issued by the Registrar, dated 8 September 1999.
6   *Cyprus v Turkey* (4 June 1999, unreported), EComHR, para 225.
7   *Cyprus v Turkey* (4 June 1999, unreported), EComHR, para 223.
8   *Cyprus v Turkey* (4 June 1999, unreported), EComHR, para 224.
9   *Ogur v Turkey* (20 May 1999, unreported), E Ct HR, para 91.

Article 3 Prohibition of torture, and of inhuman or degrading treatment or punishment

4.3.1

1   [*Contd*] However, the intention of the State in committing conduct alleged to be inhuman or degrading is a relevant factor to take into account in assessing whether the conduct violates art 3: *T v United Kingdom* 7 BHRC 659, E Ct HR (relevant that criminal proceedings against child of eleven were not intended to humiliate applicant or to cause him suffering was relevant factor to conclusion that such a trial did not violate art 3).

2   [*Contd*] See also the recent consideration of this issue by the Supreme Court of Israel in *Public Committee Against Torture v Israel* (1999) 7 BHRC 31, and the judgment of President Barak. The Court held that the use of physical means by the General Security Service ('GSS'), which impinged upon the suspect's human dignity, bodily integrity and basic rights in an excessive manner and did not serve any purpose inherent to an interrogation, was unfair and unreasonable. The Court further held that a 'necessity' or 'ticking time bomb' defence (available post factum to GSS investigators as a defence to criminal charges where the impugned act was necessary for the saving of human life) could not form the basis of authority for or justify a directive approved by a special ministerial committee authorising the use of physical means during the course of GSS interrogations.

4.3.3

6   General Assembly Resolution 3946, 10 December 1984. See paras **5.56–5.69** below, and see generally *Martinus Nijhoff* The United Nations Convention Against Torture: A Handbook on the Convention Against Torture and Other Cruel, Inhuman or Degrading Treatment or Punishment (1988) and N Rodley, The Treatment of Prisoners under International Law (1987). See also Dinah Shelton, Remedies in International Human Rights Law (1999) at pp 320–332.The definition of torture, and positive obligations imposed on states to investigate allegations of torture contained in the 1984 UN Convention, were considered as a guide to the interpretation of art 3 by the Commission and the Court in *Aydin v Turkey* (1997) 25 EHRR 251, E Ct HR. See now, for the very important consequences for signatories to the Torture Convention of the obligation to ban and outlaw torture, *R v Bow Street Metropolitan Stipendiary Magistrate, ex p Pinochet Ugarte (No 3)* [2000] 1 AC 147, HL, as distinct from the earlier decision of the House of Lords in *Pinochet Ugarte* [2000] 1 AC 61, HL, which was overturned in *Pinochet Ugarte (No 2)* [2000] 1 AC 119, HL. The House of Lords in *Pinochet Ugarte (No 3)* held that by virtue of the Convention, torture was prohibited and criminalised by international law, and hence fell beyond the legitimate functions of a head of state. Accordingly, no immunity could arise in respect of acts of torture organised or authorised by a head of state after the date upon which the relevant States had ratified and become bound by the Convention.

4.3.4

4   [*Contd*] On the other hand, where surveillance was taken to the extreme of systematically performed vaginal inspections upon prisoners' visitors, the Inter-American Commission on Human Rights held that this amounted to an infringement of the visitors' right to physical and moral integrity, and was a violation of art 5 of the Inter-American Convention: *X v Argentina* (1996) 6 BHRC 314.

4.3.6   [*Contd*] In the case of *Selmouni v France*[5], the Court acknowledged that certain acts which were classified in the past as inhuman and degrading treatment as opposed to torture could be classified differently in the future. The Court reasoned that the increasingly high standard required in the area of the protection of human rights requires greater firmness in assessing breaches of the fundamental values of democratic societies. The Court found that the beating inflicted on Mr Selmouni in custody was sufficiently severe to constitute torture.

1   *Ireland v United Kingdom* (1978) 2 EHRR 25, E Ct HR, para 167, in which the court referred to Resolution 3452 of the General Assembly of the United Nations, 9 December 1975, which declared that 'torture constitutes an aggravated and deliberate form of cruel, inhuman or degrading treatment or punishment'; *Denmark v Greece ('the Greek case')* 12 YB 186 (1972).
5   (2000) 29 EHRR 403, at para 101.

4.3.7   *[Contd]* In *Smith and Grady v United Kingdom*[5], the Court indicated that it would not exclude the possibility that treatment grounded on a predisposed bias against homosexuals could fall within the scope of art 3. However, the Court concluded that the treatment of homosexual service personnel by the Ministry of Defence, although distressing and humiliating, did not attain the minimum level of severity which would bring it within the scope of art 3.

5   (1999) 29 EHRR 493, at paras 120–122.

4.3.10   In addition, the court has imposed a positive obligation on contracting states, under arts 3 and 13 of the Convention, to carry out a prompt, impartial and effective investigation into allegations of torture, which is capable of leading to the identification and punishment of those responsible[1]. Failure to carry out such an investigation will result in a finding of a violation of art 3[2].

1   *Aksoy v Turkey* (1997) 23 EHRR 553, E Ct HR, paras 98–99; *Assenov v Bulgaria* (1998) 28 EHRR 562, E Ct HR; *Aydin v Turkey* (1997) 25 EHRR 251, E Ct HR. In imposing this positive obligation, the court referred to art 12 of the 1984 UN Convention Against Torture, which expressly provides: 'Each State Party shall ensure that its competent authorities proceed to a prompt and impartial investigation, wherever there is reasonable ground to believe that an act of torture has been committed in any territory under its jurisdiction'. See also the Inter-American Convention to Prevent and Punish Torture, art 7.
2   *Assenov v Bulgaria* (199) 28 EHRR 652, E Ct HR; *Veznedaroglu v Turkey* E Ct HR judgment of 11 April 2000.

4.3.11

3   (1998) 27 EHRR 611, E Ct HR.

4.3.13

1   *Aerts v Belgium* (1998) 29 EHRR 50, E Ct HR. The Convention does not contain an equivalent of art 10 of the International Covenant on Civil and Political Rights, which provides that: 'All persons deprived of their liberty shall be treated with humanity and with respect for the inherent dignity of the human person'. The American Convention on Human Rights contains the same provision, although it is there located within the article prohibiting torture (art 5(2)).
3   *[Contd]* See also *Blanchard v Minister of Justice, Legal and Parliamentary Affairs* [2000] 1 LRC 671 (Supreme Court of Zimbabwe).

4.3.15A   It is arguable that a sufficiently extreme minimum mandatory sentence of imprisonment may itself amount to an inhuman, cruel or degrading punishment. In *State v Likuwa*[1], the High Court of Namibia held that a minimum sentence of 10 years' imprisonment for the offence of possessing any armament (which included a rifle) without a permit infringed art 8(2)(b) of the Constitution (which is in almost identical terms to art 3 of the European Convention, with the addition of the word 'cruel'), and struck out the requirement of a minimum period of imprisonment from the legislation. See also *T v United Kingdom*[2] (punitive detention of child of eleven for six years did not violate art 3, but reference made to UN Convention on the Rights of the Child 1989, prohibiting life imprisonment without the possibility of release in respect of offences committed by persons below the age of 18).

1   [2000] 1 LRC 600.
2   7 BHRC 659, E Ct HR.

4.3.16   [*Contd*] The Privy Council held in *Thomas v Baptiste*[3] that even where the applicants were kept in appalling conditions on death row which breached the prison rules, so long as the time limits allowed in *Pratt* were complied with and since the conditions did not involve sufficient pain and suffering or such deprivation of the elementary necessities of life that they amounted to cruel and unusual punishment, there could be no commutation of the death sentence. The Court took the view that even if the conditions had constituted a breach of the appellants' constitutional rights, commutation of the sentence would be an inappropriate and disproportionate response[4].

1   [*Contd*] On 10 December 1999, the United Kingdom ratified the Second Optional Protocol to the International Covenant on Civil and Political Rights, Aiming at the Abolition of the Death Penalty (CM 4676, April 2000), which entered into force for the United Kingdom on 10 March 2000. In relation to art 3, see also *Boodram v Baptiste* [1999] 1 WLR 1709, Privy Council (Trinidad and Tobago law authorising hanging not invalidated by constitutional prohibition on cruel and unusual punishments) ; *Higgs v Minister of National Security*[2000] 2 WLR 1368 (PC). See, by contrast, *Compliance of the Death Penalty with the Constitution of the Republic of Lithuania* 6 BHRC 283 (1998), where the Constitutional Court of Lithuania held that the death penalty infringed the prohibition contained in art 21(3) of the Constitution on acts which could be shown to 'torture, injure, degrade or maltreat' a person, as well as infringing the right to life under art 19.
3   [1999] 3 WLR 249.
4   Cf *Higgs v Minister of National Security* [2000] 2 WLR 1368 (PC).

4.3.17

1   [*Contd*] *Thomas v Baptiste* [1999] 3 WLR 249; *Higgs v Minister of National Security* [2000] 2 WLR 1368 (PC).

4.3.19

2   [*Contd*] See *Elmi v Australia* (1999) 6 BHRC 433, where the UN Committee found that there were substantial grounds for believing that a person would be in danger of torture if returned to Somalia. The Committee appeared to accept that it was for that person to show that the acts of torture would be carried out by a 'public official or any other person acting in an official capacity' (within art 1 of the Convention), but held that Somalia's warring factions were capable of constituting public officials.

4.3.20

1   [*Contd*] *Ould Barar v Sweden* Application 42367/98, Decision of 19 January 1999: alleged risk of (private) punishment as an 'escaped slave'; application held to be manifestly ill-founded, despite criticisms of steps taken by Mauritanian Government. But see *Elmi v Australia*, above.

4.5
Article 5 Right to liberty and security of person

4.5.15 [*Contd*] In *Steel v United Kingdom*[7] the Court considered that detention for refusing to be bound over to keep the peace fell within art 5(1)(b) since it was imposed as a result of the applicants' non-compliance with a lawful court order. Whilst the order was 'expressed in rather vague and general terms' the Court was satisfied, given the factual circumstances, that the applicants understood the nature of the conduct which was prohibited[8].

7   (1998) 28 EHRR 603.
8   Cf *Hashman and Harrap v United Kingdom* [2000] Crim LR 185, E Ct HR where a bindover requiring the applicants to be 'of good behaviour' was held by the E Ct HR to be insufficiently specific to qualify as law, since it failed to provide any objective criteria against which their past and future conduct could be judged.

4.5.22 [*Contd*] In *Steel v United Kingdom*[7] the Court held that 'breach of the peace' fell to be regarded as a criminal offence for the purposes of art 5(1)(c). Whilst it was not so regarded in English law, the Court emphasised that the obligation to keep the peace was in the nature of a public duty, that an actual or threatened breach of the peace gave rise to a power of arrest, and that a refusal to be bound over could result in imprisonment.

7   (1998) 28 EHRR 603.

4.5.26 Article 5(1)(e) authorises the detention by lawful order of persons for the prevention of the spreading of infectious diseases, of persons of unsound mind, alcoholics, drug addicts or vagrants. In general, persons falling into any of these categories may be detained not only for reasons of public safety, but also because their own interests may necessitate their detention: the clause contemplates inter alia the social protection of vulnerable groups[1]. There have been no cases before the E Ct HR or Commission dealing with the prevention of the spread of infectious diseases, or of the detention of alcoholics or drug addicts[1a]. However, the cases relating to persons of unsound mind, and vagrants, provided some general guidance as to the operation of the clause.

1   [*Contd*] See also *Witold Litwa v Poland* (E Ct HR, Judgment 4 April 2000), at para 60.
1a   But see now *Witold Litwa v Poland*, where the E Ct HR held that detention of the Applicant in Krakow Sobering-up Centre was, on the facts, a violation of art 5(1)(e). The Court held that although the word 'alcoholics' in its common usage denotes persons who are addicted to alcohol, the term as used in art 5(1)(e) was not limited to the detention of persons who were in a clinical state of 'alcoholism, but extended to persons whose conduct and behaviour under the influence of alcohol was such as to pose a threat to public order or themselves. Such persons could be taken into custody for the protection of the public or their own interests: Judgment, paras 60–61. On the facts, however, the detention of the applicant was unlawful because, even though drunk, it could not be said that he posed a threat to the public or to himself. However, decision will, it is suggested, give a basis for the lawful detention of intoxicated football supporters, even where there is no evidence of long term alcoholism.

4.5.27

4   [*Contd*] In *Johnson v United Kingdom* (1999) 27 EHRR 296, the E Ct HR considered in detail the operation of this third rule, and the obligations of a State where an individual is found no longer to

suffer from a mental disorder warranting confinement. The Court held that where this occurs, the State is not under an immediate and unconditional obligation to release the patient; rather (particularly having regard to the fact that mental illness is an inexact science), the State is entitled to proceed with caution and to take time to consider whether to terminate the confinement. Further, the State is entitled to retain some measure of supervision over the patient once released (such as a period of rehabilitation in a hostel, at least in circumstances where the recurrence of the mental illness cannot be excluded), and may be entitled to delay release until conditions for such supervision are put in place. However, there is an obligation upon the State to put such conditions into place within a reasonable time, and in this respect the Court held that there was on the facts a violation of art 5(1)(e).

5   *Winterwerp v Netherlands* (1979) 2 EHRR 387, para 40. Indeed, there have been no cases in which any of the three tests laid down in *Winterwerp* have been held to be violated. But see now, *Johnson v United Kingdom* (above), where the Court found a violation of the third test; see also, *Aerts v Belgium* (2000) 29 EHRR 50 (provisional detention in psychiatric wing of ordinary prison for eight months, awaiting decision of Mental Health Board, violated art 5(1)(e)). See also *Luberti v Italy* (1984) 6 EHRR 440; *X v United Kingdom* (1982) 4 EHRR 188 (criteria apply to recall of patient).

4.5.28   Article 5(1)(e) does not govern conditions of confinement or govern the provision of suitable treatment, which are matters for art 3[1]. However in *Ashingdane v United Kingdom*[2], the E Ct HR held that the detention of persons[2a] of unsound mind is required to be in a hospital, clinic, or other appropriate institution authorised for the detention of such persons. No definition of 'unsound mind' has been attempted by the E Ct HR or Commission, but it has been emphasised that the deprivation of a person's liberty cannot be justified simply because his views or behaviour deviate from the norms prevailing in a particular society[3].

2a   And see now *Aerts v Belgium* (2000) 29 EHRR 50, where the E Ct HR followed *Ashingdane* in holding (at para 48) that detention in the psychiatric wing of an ordinary hospital did not constitute detention in a hospital, clinic or other appropriate institution (in circumstances in which it was accepted that the applicant's treatment had not been therapeutically satisfactory).

4.5.31

3   [*Contd*] See further, for examples of detention held not to be arbitrary, and the wide discretion accorded to Member States, *Gonzalez v Spain* (Application 43544/98, 29 June 1999; declared inadmissible); *Shkelzen v Germany* (Application 44770/98, 21 January 2000; declared inadmissible); *Aslan v Malta* (Application 29493/95, 3 February 2000; declared inadmissible).

4.5.32

4   [*Contd*] Compare *Dougoz v Greece* (Application 40907/98, 8 February 2000; declared admissible on this ground), where detention for 18 months in allegedly poor conditions was held to give rise to an admissible complaint.

4.5.40

5   [*Contd*] The detention of service personnel pending a court martial by order of the commanding officer does not meet the requirements of art 5(3): *Hood v United Kingdom* (1999) 29 EHRR 365, E Ct HR); *Jordan v United Kingdom* E Ct HR, Times, 17 March (2000).

4.5.41

2   [*Contd*] In *Caballero v United Kingdom* [2000] Crim LR 587, E Ct HR the Government conceded in the E Ct HR that s 25 of the Criminal Justice and Public Order Act 1994 (prohibition on the grant of bail for certain serious offences, where defendant has relevant previous conviction) was in breach of art 5(3).

4.5.56   [*Contd*] In *T and V v United Kingdom*[3], the Court held that the fixing of a tariff for a young person detained at Her Majesty's Pleasure is a sentencing exercise, such that the procedure whereby the tariff was fixed by the Home Secretary constituted a violation of art 6(1). In the light of that finding, and of the fact that the applicants' tariff had been quashed by the House of Lords, the Court concluded that the failure to refer their case to the Parole Board amounted to a violation of art 5(4).

3   [2000] Crim LR 187, E Ct HR.

4.6
Article 6 Right to a fair trial

4.6.1

2 [*Contd*] Note that the art 6 right to the fair administration of justice may be violated by encroachments upon legal professional privilege: see *R v Middlesex Guildhall Crown Court, ex p Tamosius & Partners* [2000] 1 WLR 453, QBD, *per* Moses J at 459, *R v Derby Magistrates' Court, ex p B* [1996] AC 487, HL, at 507 and *Niemietz v Germany* (1992) 16 EHRR 97, E Ct HR, at 114. See also *General Mediterranean Holdings v Patel* [2000] 1 WLR 272, QBD.

4.6.3

1 [*Contd*] See also *Pafitis v Greece* (1999) 27 EHRR 566, E Ct HR, para 87 (applicant shareholders had an arguable claim under domestic and European Community law to the right to participate in bank's decisions concerning share value). The principle stated in the main text was applied by the English Court of Appeal in *R v Lord Chancellor, ex p Lightfoot* [2000] 2 WLR 318, *per* Simon Brown LJ at 332.

4.6.5

2 [*Contd*] For a further example of the application of this principle, see *MS v Sweden* (1998) 28 EHRR 313, E Ct HR, paras 49–50 (no arguable right in national law to prevent communication of confidential medical data: held, art 6(1) inapplicable).

3 *Fayed v United Kingdom* (1994) 18 EHRR 393, E Ct HR, para 65; *Tinnelly and McElduff v United Kingdom* (1998) 27 EHRR 249, E Ct HR, para 62 (operation of national security certificates barring further proceedings in Fair Employment Tribunal fell to be examined under art 6(1).

4 See *Fayed v United Kingdom* (1994) 18 EHRR 393, E Ct HR, at para 67, and *Osman v United Kingdom*, (2000) 29 EHRR 245, paras 133–140 (police immunity from common law negligence claims: E Ct HR rejected respondent Government's argument that applicants had no substantive right for purposes of applicability of art 6(1)). See also Application 28945/95 *TP and KM v United Kingdom*, EComHR Report of 26 May 1998 (local authority's immunity from suit in negligence in child care cases: complaints under art 6(1) declared inadmissible); *Waite and Kennedy v Germany* (1999) 6 BHRC 499, paras 63–74 (international organisation's immunity from suit in employment litigation: no violation of art 6(1) because immunity pursued a legitimate aim and did not, in the circumstances, breach principle of proportionality. The Commission returned to the problems of exclusionary rules in English tort law (raised by the *Osman* case in *Z v UK*, EComHR, report of September 1999 (striking out of negligence claim against local authority social workers on the ground that not fair, just and reasonable to impose a duty of care, in *X v Bedfordshire County Council* [1995] AC 633, HL, violated art 6(1)). For consideration of *Osman* and its progeny by the English courts, see *Barrett v London Borough of Enfield* [1999] 3 WLR 79, HL, *Gower v London Borough of Bromley* [1999] ELR 356, CA, *A & B v Gloucestershire County Council* (14 March 2000, unreported), CA and *Phelps v Hillingdon London Borough Council* (2000) Times, 28 July, HL. The E Ct HR has ruled admissible a number of recent applications alleging that sovereign or state immunity violates the right of access to a court in art 6: see *Fogarty v United Kingdom* (1 March 2000, unreported) E Ct HR; *Al-Adsani v United Kingdom* (1 March 2000, unreported) E Ct HR; *McElhinney v Ireland and United Kingdom* (9 February 2000, unreported) E Ct HR. Cf *Holland v Lampen-Wolfe* [1999] 1 WLR 188, CA; affd [2000] 1 WLR 1573.

4.6.6

5 [*Contd*] If an applicant has failed even to attempt to bring civil proceedings in the domestic courts, his claim under art 6(1) may be rejected as speculative: see eg *Assenov v Bulgaria* (1999) 28 EHRR 652, E Ct HR, para 112.

4.6.7   Proceedings for the enforcement of a settlement agreement may also be 'decisive' of a civil right[1].

1   *Pérez de Rada Cavanilles v Spain* (2000) 29 EHRR 109, E Ct HR, para 39.

4.6.8

1   [*Contd*] For further analysis of the E Ct HR's distinction between private and public law rights, see Herberg, Le Sueur and Mulcahy, *Fundamental Human Rights Principles: Defining the Limits to Rights*, to be published by Justice. The authors argue that the distinction is 'open to serious question' and that the intention of the framers of the Convention was simply to use the term 'civil' in contradistinction to 'criminal' in the same sentence: see further Van Dijk, *The interpretation of 'civil rights and obligations' by the European Court of Human Rights – one more step to take*, at p 131 in *Protecting Human Rights: The European Dimension* (Studies in honour of Gerard J Wiarda, 1990) and Newman, *Natural Justice, Due Process and the New International Covenants on Human Rights: Prospectus* [1967] *Public Law* 274.

4.6.10

1   [*Contd*] See also *Vasilescu v Romania* (1999) 28 EHRR 241, E Ct HR (action for recovery of property confiscated by the State).
6   [*Contd*] See also *Aerts v Belgium* (1998) 29 EHRR 50, E Ct HR, para 59 (the right to liberty of a person detained, following arrest, in the psychiatric wing of a prison was a 'civil right', apparently because the applicant was seeking a judicial declaration that the domestic court had jurisdiction to award him compensation for unlawful imprisonment).

4.6.11

4   [*Contd*] The E Ct HR has recently recognised that its case-law on civil servants 'contains a margin of uncertainty' and has sought to apply a new 'functional criterion' based on employees' duties and responsibilities, with only employees in posts involving participation in the exercise of powers conferred by public law falling outside the scope of art 6: see *Pellegrin v France*, E Ct HR, judgment of 8 December 1999 at paras 64–67 (reflecting eg the dissenting opinion of Judge Pekkanen in *Argento v Italy* (1999) 28 EHRR 719, E Ct HR). The Court further held (at para 67), however, that *all* disputes involving pensions fell within art 6(1) 'because on retirement employees break the special bond between themselves and the authorities': for a recent example in this category, see *McGinley and Egan v United Kingdom* (1999) 27 EHRR 1, E Ct HR, at para 84.

4.6.13   [*Contd*] Proceedings in England and Wales whereby a defendant may be bound over to keep the peace[9] or to be of good behaviour[10] involve the determination of a criminal charge.

9   *Steel v United Kingdom* (1998) 28 EHRR 603, E Ct HR.
10   *Hashman and Harrap v United Kingdom*, [2000] Crim LR 185, E Ct HR.

4.6.16

1   [*Contd*] Cf *R v Lord Chancellor, ex p Lightfoot* [2000] 2 WLR 318 (mandatory deposit payable by debtor wishing to petition for bankruptcy did not infringe any constitutional right). As to the compatibility with art 6 of a stay of proceedings pending the outcome of an arbitration abroad, see *Reichhold Norway ASA v Goldman Sachs International* [2000] 1 WLR 173, CA.

4.6.17

1   [*Contd*] See further *Aerts v Belgium* (2000) 29 EHRR 50, E Ct HR, para 60 (right to liberty of prisoner: refusal of legal aid by Legal Aid Board on ground that appeal did not appear to be well-founded violated art 6(1) because it was for the Court, not the Legal Aid Board, to assess the proposed appeal's prospects of success); *Faulkner v United Kingdom* Times, 11 January 2000, E Ct HR (friendly settlement on basis that United Kingdom government would introduce legal aid scheme

for Guernsey: Court summarised its previous case-law to the effect that the costs and expenses related to the institution of proceedings should not effectively bar access to court for impecunious litigants). See *too R v Secretary of State for the Environment, Transport and the Regions, ex p Challenger* (2000) Times, 11 July.

4.6.18

2   [*Contd*] For a case where the strict application of a short limitation period did impair the very essence of the right of access to a court, see *Pérez de Rada Cavanilles v Spain* (2000) 29 EHRR 109, E Ct HR, paras 43–50. For recent consideration of a similar issue by the ECJ, see *Levez v T H Jennings* C-326/96 [1999] IRLR 36. See also *Omar v France* (2000) 29 EHRR 210, E Ct HR, paras 40–44 (automatic bar to appeal on point of law that convicted appellant had failed to surrender to custody pursuant to arrest warrant: held, applying *Poitrimol v France* (1994) 18 EHRR 130, E Ct HR, disproportionate restriction on right of access) and *Canea Catholic Church v Greece* (1999) 27 EHRR 521, E Ct HR, paras 34–42 (Court's holding, contrary to 'settled case law and administrative practice', that church had no legal personality, violated art 6(1)).

4.6.19

1   [*Contd*] See also *Ebert v Venvil* [1999] 3 WLR 670, CA (court had inherent power to restrict actions by vexatious litigant, and requirements of art 6 did no more than reflect the common law); *Johnson v Valks*, [2000] 1 All ER 450, CA (question of leave to appeal for a vexatious litigant was important in view of coming into force of the Human Rights Act 1998).

5   [*Contd*] For the application of art 6 to striking-out under the Civil Procedure Rules, see *Arrow Nominees v Blackledge* (1999) Times, 8 December Ch D; (2000) Times, 7 July, CA. See also *In re Swaptronics Ltd* Times, 17 August 1998.

4.6.21

2   [*Contd*] See also *Kaya v Turkey* (1999) 28 EHRR1, E Ct HR, para 105 and *Vasilescu v Romania* (1999) 28 EHRR 241, E Ct HR, para 43 (in civil cases, art 6(1) is a *lex specialis* in relation to art 13).

4.6.22   The manner in which art 6 applies to courts of appeal will depend upon the features of the proceedings concerned, and account must be taken of the entirety of the domestic proceedings and the appeal court's role therein[1].

1   *JJ v The Netherlands* (1999) 28 EHRR 168, E Ct HR, para 38. See also para **4.6.30**.

4.6.24

3   *Bryan v United Kingdom* (1995) 21 EHRR 342, E Ct HR, at para 45, applied by the EComHR (in each case rejecting the applicant's complaints) in *X v United Kingdom*, decision of 19 January 1998; Application 29419/95 *Stefan v United Kingdom* (1997) 25 EHRR CD 130, see further *Stefan v General Medical Council* [1999] 1 WLR 1293, PC; *APB and others v United Kingdom*, 91998) 25 EHRR CD 141, E Ct HR and *Wickramsinghe v United Kingdom*, decision of 9 December 1997.

4.6.30

1   [*Contd*] See similarly *JJ v The Netherlands* (1999) 28 EHRR 168, E Ct HR, paras 38–41.

4.6.31   As to the language in which civil proceedings should be conducted, see *Williams v Cowell*[1] (no violation of art 6, taken alone or with art 14, where EAT in London refused to conduct proceedings in Welsh as appellant could speak and understand English).

1   [2000] 1 WLR 187, CA.

4.6.32 [*Contd*] In *Rowe and Davis v United Kingdom*[5], the Court held that considerations of national security or the protection of vulnerable witnesses may, in certain circumstances, justify an exception to this rule. Any departure from the principles of open adversarial justice must however be strictly necessary, and the consequent handicap imposed on the defence must be adequately counterbalanced by procedural safeguards to protect the rights of the accused[6]. Article 6(1) also implies the ability of an accused to understand and participate effectively in a criminal trial[7]. Where juveniles are tried in the Crown Court for murder or other serious offences, art 6 requires a specially adapted procedure which promotes the welfare of the young defendant, adequately respects his right to privacy, and enables him to understand and participate fully in the proceedings[8].

5   [2000] Crim LR 584.
6   Where the prosecution had withheld relevant evidence on public interest immunity grounds, without first submitting the material to the trial judge, the requirements of art 6 were not met; and the resulting defect could not be cured by submitting the material to the Court of Appeal in the course of an appeal against conviction. *C Fitt and Jasper v United Kingdom* (16 February 2000, unreported), where the Court held, by a majority of nine to eight, that there was no violation of art 6 where the material in question had been submitted to the trial judge under the *ex parte* procedure established in *R v Davis, Johnson and Rowe* (1993) 97 Cr App Rep 110.
7   *Stanford v United Kingdom* (1994) Series A No 282-A.
8   *T and V v United Kingdom* [2000] Crim LR 187, E Ct HR. As to the procedure to be followed at trial in the light of the Court's judgment, see *Practice Direction (Crown Court: Trial of Children and Young Persons)* [2000] 2 All ER 284. The guiding principle is that the trial should not expose the young defendant to avoidable intimidation, humiliation or distress, and should be conducted with regard to the welfare of the child or young person.

4.6.33 [*Contd*] There will be a violation of the right to a fair hearing if a respondent State, without good cause, prevents an applicant from gaining access to, or falsely denies the existence of, documents in its possession which are of assistance to the applicant's case[5].

3   [*Contd*] See also *JJ v The Netherlands* (1999) 28 EHRR 168, E Ct HR (lack of opportunity to reply to Advocate General's decision: cf, in relation to the ECJ, *Emesa Sugar (Free Zone) NV v Aruba* Case C-17/98, ECJ, (Times, 29 February 2000). For domestic application of these principles, see *Nwabueze v General Medical Council* [2000] 2 All ER 285 (art 6 and the common law both required the same thing, namely that parties should have a chance of addressing tribunal on advice given by legal assessor).
5   *McGinley and Egan v United Kingdom* (1999) 27 EHRR 1, E Ct HR, para 86. See also main text, para **4.6.33**, n 3.

4.6.35

2   [*Contd*] *Khan v United Kingdom* (2000) Times, 23 May, E Ct HR.

4.6.36 [*Contd*] The House of Lords considered the implications of these decisions in *R v Hertfordshire County Council, ex p Green Environmental Industries Ltd*[3]. The protection against self-incrimination, as it was understood in Saunders, was relevant only where the prosecution sought to introduce evidence obtained by powers of compulsory questioning in the course of a criminal trial. Under the HRA 1998 it would be incumbent on a judge to consider whether art 6(1) required the exclusion of such evidence. Article 6 did not, however, prevent the use of compulsory questioning powers during the investigative phase of an inquiry.

1   [*Contd*] As to the admissibility of evidence obtained by compulsion in non-criminal cases, see *Official Receiver v Stern*, Judgment of 2 February 2000, CA (use of evidence obtained by legal compulsion under s 235 of Insolvency Act 1986 in disqualification proceedings did not necessarily involve breach of art 6; issues of admissibility of evidence in a particular case were best considered by trial Judge, considering the relevant factors in the round).

3   [2000] 1 All ER 773, HL (per Lord Hoffman at 781D *et seq*).

4.6.37   [*Contd*] In *Condron and Condron v United Kingdom*[4], the European Court of Human Rights held that the direction given to the jury had failed to strike the balance required by art 6. In particular, the jury should have been directed, as a matter of fairness, that if the applicants' silence at interview could not attributed to their having no answer, or none that would stand up to cross-examination, then no adverse inference should be drawn[5].

4   (2000) Times, 9 May, E Ct HR.

5   The unfairness which resulted from such a misdirection could not be cured on appeal. Whilst it was possible, in some cases, for a defect at trial to be remedied at the appellate level (*Edwards v United Kingdom* (1992) 15 EHRR 417) that was not the position in the present case, since Court of Appeal had no means of knowing whether the applicants' silence played a significant role in the jury's decision to convict them.

4.6.39

3   [*Contd*] Similarly, in *Higgins v France* (1999) 27 EHRR 703, E Ct HR, para 43, a violation of art 6(1) was found where the national court had given no reasons for rejecting an application to transfer to another court on the grounds of bias, while allowing such applications in two related sets of proceedings. As to bias generally, see paras **4.6.52–58**.

4.6.40

1   [*Contd*] As to the right of a non-party to inspect court documents, see *GIO Personal Investment Services Ltd v Liverpool and London Steamship Protection and Indemnity Association* [1999] 1 WLR 984, CA.

4.6.41   [*Contd*] If none of the express restrictions set out in the text of the article applies, a violation will be found[4].

1   [*Contd*] See also *R v Bow County Court, ex p Pelling* [1999] 1 WLR 1807, DC, *per* Otton LJ at 1815–6 (exclusion of *McKenzie* friend from family proceedings in chambers did not violate art 6).

4   *Gautrin v France* (1999) 28 EHRR 196, E Ct HR, paras 42–43 (violation where medical professional disciplinary hearings not held in public).

4.6.48   [*Contd*] Note that a fair balance is to be struck between the requirement that judicial proceedings should be conducted expeditiously and the more general principle of the proper administration of justice (also derived from art 6(1))[4].

4   See eg *Pafitis v Greece* (1999) 27 EHRR 566, E Ct HR, para 97.

4.6.49

1   [*Contd*] Note also that in *Pafitis v Greece* (1999) 27 EHRR 566, E Ct HR, para 96, delays caused by a strike by members of the Athens Bar were held to be attributable to the State.

4.6.51A   For the principle of bias in English law, see *R v Gough*[1]; *R v Bow Street Metropolitan Stipendiary Magistrate, ex p Pinochet Ugarte (No 2)*[2]; *Locabail (UK) Ltd v Bayfield Properties*[3]; *Nwabueze v General Medical Council* PC, 6

April 2000, transcript at p 11; *A T & T v Saudi Cable*; *R v Chief Constable of Merseyside Police, ex p Bennion*. The domestic courts are already showing themselves willing to apply Convention principles to the issue of whether a tribunal is sufficiently independent and/or impartial[4].

1   [1993] AC 646, HL.
2   [1999] 2 WLR 272, HL.
3   [2000] 1 All ER 65.
4   [2000] 1 All ER (Comm) 201.
5   (2000) Times, 18 July.
6   See *Smith v Secretary of State for Trade and Industry* [2000] IRLR 6, EAT (EAT granting leave to appeal to CA to allow applicant to argue the 'real and troubling question' of whether, given respondent Secretary of State's powers of appointment etc in relation to lay members, Employment Tribunal not independent/impartial for Convention purposes when determining claims against him. The appeal was not, however, pursued); *Starrs v Procurator Fiscal, Linlithgow*, 1999 SCCR 1052, High Court of Justiciary (judicial appointment system for deputy sheriffs, who lacked security of tenure, meant breach of art 6 independence requirement); *Jiad v BBC World Service* [2000] ICR Recent Points Part 3 p xi, EAT (while it was undesirable that tribunal members should be called to give oral evidence where bias was alleged, it was not a matter of policy that they should never be ordered to do so: such a policy would lead to the issue not being dealt with fairly, contrary to the requirement of a fair trial in domestic law and under art 6).

4.6.54

5   [*Contd*] *Findlay v United Kingdom* was applied in *Hood v United Kingdom* (2000) 29 EHRR 365, E Ct HR, paras 73–79. Cf *R v Martin (Alan)* [1998] AC 917, HL.
6   *Campbell and Fell v United Kingdom* (1984) 7 EHRR 165, E Ct HR, at para 81 (requirement of independence not infringed by Board of Visitors, because prisoners were not 'reasonably entitled' to believe the Board to be dependent upon the executive). In *McGonnell v United Kingdom*, EComHR Report of 20 October 1998, the EComHR held that the position of the Bailiff in Guernsey, who was 'not only a senior member of the judiciary of the island, but was also a senior member of the legislature … and, in addition, a senior member of the executive' was incompatible with the requirement of an appearance of independence. See also *Incal v Turkey* (2000) 29 EHRR 449, E Ct HR, paras 65–73. The E Ct HR in the *McGonnell v United Kingdom* case (2000) Times, 22 February, similarly found a violation of the requirements of independence and impartiality, holding that any direct involvement in the passage of legislation, or of executive rules, was likely to cast doubt on the judicial impartiality of a person who subsequently determined a dispute over whether reasons existed to permit a variation from the wording of the legislation or rules at issue. Note the potential consequences of this decision in relation to the constitutional roles of the Lord Chancellor and the Law Lords. See also *Khan v United Kingdom* (2000) Times, 23 May, E Ct HR (Police Complaints Authority did not provide sufficient guarantees of independence for the purposes of art 13); *R v X, Y and Z* (2000) Times, 23 May, CA.

4.6.56   [*Contd*] Executive involvement in sentencing is incompatible with art 6. In *T and V v United Kingdom*[6] the Court held that the fixing of a tariff period to be served by a juvenile convicted of murder and sentenced to detention at Her Majesty's Pleasure under s 53(1) of the Children and Young Persons Act 1933 is a sentencing exercise, which attracts the guarantees of art 6. Accordingly, it was a breach of the independence requirement in art 6(1) for the tariff period to be set by a member of the executive.

3   [*Contd*] See, similarly, *Gautrin v France* (1999) 28 EHRR 196, E Ct HR, paras 57–60 (doctors' disciplinary tribunal not 'impartial' in circumstances of case because of its 'worrying connection' with the competitors of the applicants' organisation, SOS Médecins).
6   (1999) Times, 12 May.

4.6.57

1   [*Contd*] See also *Sander v United Kingdom* (2000) Times, 12 May (legitimate doubt about racism in the jury room not capable of being dispelled by a judicial direction, however strongly it was worded).

4.6.59 [*Contd*] The application of these principles to statutory reverse onus provisions in England and Wales was considered by Lord Hope in *R v DPP, ex p Kebilene*[5]. The court should determine whether the legislative technique which had been adopted imposed a persuasive or merely evidential burden, whether it was mandatory or discretionary, and whether it related to an essential element of the offence, or merely to an exemption or proviso. In considering a mandatory persuasive burden on an important essential element, the question for the court would be whether the presumption was confined within reasonable limits. In determining that issue a court might usefully consider three questions:

(1) What does the prosecution have to prove in order to transfer the onus to the defence?
(2) Does the burden imposed on the accused relate to something which is likely to be difficult for him to prove, or does it relate to something which is likely to be within his knowledge or to which he has ready access?
(3) What is the nature of the threat faced by society which the provision is designed to combat?

5 [1999] 3 WLR 972 HL.

4.6.61 Similarly, a refusal to order the payment of costs to an acquitted defendant will violate the presumption of innocence if the ground for the refusal reflects a suspicion that the accused is guilty. In *Minelli v Switzerland*[1] the E Ct HR found a violation of art 6(2) where an acquitted defendant had been ordered to pay costs on the basis that he would 'very probably' have been convicted had he not been saved by the operation of a limitation period for the offence[2].

1 (1983) 5 EHRR 554.
2 In order to give effect to this principle the *Practice Direction (Costs in Criminal Proceedings)* (1991) 93 Cr App Rep 89 has been amended so as to delete para 2(2)(b) which permitted the refusal of defence costs on the ground that there was ample evidence to support a conviction but the accused had been acquitted on a technicality which had no merit: *Practice Direction (Crime: Costs in Criminal Proceedings) (No 2)*, Times, 6 October 1999.

4.6.80 This provision embodies the prohibition on double jeopardy in criminal cases which is reflected in the English pleas in bar of *autrefois convict* and *autrefois acquit*. The Commission has in the past left open the question whether the right to a fair hearing in art 6 already incorporates this protection[1], but in *S v Federal Republic of Germany*[2] the Commission held that art 6 guarantees 'neither expressly nor by way of implication the principle of *ne bis in idem*'. The extent of the protection provided by art 4 of the seventh protocol is qualified. It is confined to prosecutions in the same jurisdiction, and so does not prevent successive prosecutions for the same offence in different countries[3]. Nor does it prevent separate disciplinary and criminal proceedings in respect of the same allegation. In *Gradinger v Austria*[4] the E Ct HR held that there had been a violation of art 4 where the applicant had been convicted and sentenced for a criminal offence of causing death by negligent driving and the administrative authorities subsequently fined him for driving under the influence of alcohol[5]. Although the elements of the two offences were different, they were 'based on the same conduct'[6].

1 *X v Austria* 35 CD 151 (1970). The Commission held that the fact that express protection against double jeopardy was provided by protocol 7 did not necessarily mean that such protection was not inherent in art 6 for those states which were not parties to the protocol.

Article 6   Right to a fair trial

2   Cf *S v Federal Republic of Germany* 39 DR 43 (1983).
3   Cf *S v Federal Republic of Germany* 39 DR 43 (1983).
4   (1995) Series A/328-C.
5   The E Ct HR assumed that the administrative proceedings were 'criminal' for the purpose of art 4 of the seventh protocol, having found that they were 'criminal' for the purpose of art 6.
6   The implications of art 4 of Protocol 7 were extensively considered by the Law Commission in Consultation Paper No 156 *Double Jeopardy* (1999).

4.8

Article 8 Right to respect for private and family life, home and correspondence

4.8.4

6   [*Contd*] See also *McGinley and Egan v United Kingdom* (1998) 27 EHRR 1, E Ct HR, para 99 (access to information for ex-servicemen stationed on or near Christmas Island at the time of British nuclear tests in 1958), distinguishing *Guerra v Italy*. It was held, by five votes to four, that there was no violation.

4.8.7 [*Contd*] The controversial issue of whether companies and other legal personalities have privacy rights under art 8 has been left open by the Court of Appeal in *R v Broadcasting Standards Commission, ex p BBC*[3]. However, privacy rights for such bodies were found for the company, Dixons, under the domestic legislation in question; see also *Cantabrica Coach Holdings Ltd v Vehicle Inspectorate*[4] where the art 8 point was again left open. For the ECJ's and CFI's approach to this issue, see *Limburgse Vinyl Maatschappij NV & 11 other PVC Producers v EC Commission*[5].

3   [2000] 17 LS Gaz R 32.
4   [2000] 18 LS Gaz R 37, DC.
5   CFI, 20 April 1999, [1999] ECR II- (to be reported), paras 396–423.

4.8.9 [*Contd*] *Osman v United Kingdom* shows that the notion of 'respect' may entail a positive obligation on the part of the state to secure an applicant's physical integrity or safety from foreseeable criminal attack[10]. Equally, such a positive obligation may extend to using the criminal law to protect an individual from harassment[11]. *McGinley and Egan v United Kingdom* also brought within art 8 the positive obligation to confer a right of access to information which could either allay health fears or better enable an individual to assess a health risk. The E Ct HR held that where a government engages in hazardous activities which might have hidden adverse consequences for the health of those involved, art 8 requires that an effective and accessible procedure be established to enable such persons to seek all relevant and appropriate information[12].

1   [*Contd*] The failure of domestic law to provide the right for children in local authority care to sue the authority in negligence for the failure to protect them from severe ill-treatment by their parents of which the authority was aware was the context of *Z v United Kingdom* (1999) 28 EHRR CD 65, EComHR. The immunity was conferred on local authorities by the House of Lords in the antecedent domestic proceedings: *X (Minors) v Bedfordshire County Council* [1995] 2 AC 633. The children complained that the ill-treatment disclosed a serious infringement of their moral and physical integrity contrary to art 8(1). The EComHR concluded at 272 that there had been a violation of art 3 but that no separate issue arose under art 8. The case has been referred to the E Ct HR. Judgment is still pending. The forcible examination of a mentally handicapped person in hospital is an interference with that person's private life: *Matter v Slovakia*, judgment 5 July 1999, E Ct HR, para 64.
5   [*Contd*] *A v United Kingdom* is now reported at (1998) 27 EHRR 611, E Ct HR.
7   [*Contd*] See also *McGinley and Egan v United Kingdom* (1998) 27 EHRR 1, E Ct HR, para 99 (access to information for ex-servicemen stationed on or near Christmas Island at the time of British nuclear tests in 1958), distinguishing *Guerra v Italy*. It was held, by five votes to four, that there was no violation.

10 *Osman v United Kingdom* (1998) 29 EHRR 245, E Ct HR, para 128. On the facts, no violation was found because the police response as events unfolded was reasonable in all the circumstances.
11 (1998) 29 EHRR 245, E Ct HR, paras 129–130. Indeed, in appropriate circumstances the positive obligation may require the creation of a civil remedy in damages for harassment: see *Whiteside v United Kingdom* (1994) 18 EHRR CD 126, EComHR. The Protection from Harassment Act 1997 provides for both criminal and civil liability for harassment and should be interpreted (under the HRA 1998, s 3(1)) consistently with these obligations.
12 (1998) 27 EHRR 1, E Ct HR, paras 96–98 and 101 (withholding information from ex-servicemen stationed on or near Christmas Island at the time of British nuclear tests in 1958). It was held, paras 102–104, that there had been no violation of the positive obligation because a procedure for seeking the information applied under the Pensions Appeal Tribunal Rules but the applicants had failed to use it.

4.8.11

1 [*Contd*] See also *R v Broadcasting Standards Commission, ex p BBC* [2000] 17 LS Gaz R 32, CA.

4.8.13

4 [*Contd*] See also the analysis by Lord Clyde in *Fitzpatrick v Sterling Housing Association* [1999] 3 WLR 1113; and see also *R v Secretary of State for the Home Department, ex p Fielding* (Latham J, 5 July 1999) (1999) Times, 21 July where a policy limiting the supply of condoms to homosexual prisoners was held to be a potential interference with art 8 rights.

4.8.13A   The legality of the Ministry of Defence's policy that homosexuality was, in itself, incompatible with service in the armed forces was examined by the E Ct HR in *Smith and Grady v United Kingdom*[1] and *Lustig-Prean and Beckett v United Kingdom*[2]. It held:

(1) The investigations and report into the applicants' sexual orientation and practices and their discharge from the armed forces constituted direct and especially grave interferences with their right to respect for their private life within art 8(1).
(2) As regards art 8(2), these actions were 'in accordance with the law' because they complied with the applicable domestic and European Union law.
(3) The actions pursued the legitimate aims of 'the interests of national security' and 'the prevention of disorder'.
(4) But they were not 'necessary in a democratic society' because they were not proportionate to the legitimate aims. In this respect, the E Ct HR emphasised that the hallmarks of a 'democratic society' included pluralism, tolerance and broadmindedness.
(5) While the national authorities had to make the initial assessment and while a margin of appreciation was left open to them, where the interference concerns a most intimate part of an individual's life there must exist particularly weighty and convincing reasons before such an interference can satisfy art 8(2).
(6) While rules can be imposed to preserve the morale and to ensure the operational effectiveness of the armed forces, assertions of a threat to morale and operational effectiveness must be backed by specific examples.
(7) In the present cases, although some difficulties could be anticipated, there was insufficient concrete evidence of such threats. In particular, the E Ct HR was not persuaded that conduct codes and disciplinary rules of the type used effectively to combat racial discrimination and racial and sexual harassment and bullying could not be equally effective in dealing with ill-treatment of homosexuals by colleagues.

(8) The E Ct HR stressed that those European countries which maintained an outright ban on homosexuals serving in the armed forces were now in a small minority.

(9) It also stressed that the continuation of the applicants' questioning after their admission of homosexuality could not be justified.

(10) It held, therefore, that neither the investigations into the applicant's sexual orientation and practices nor the consequential report nor their forced discharge from the armed forces could be justified under art 8(2).

7   (1999) 29 EHRR 493, paras 71–112.
8   (1999) 29 EHRR 548, paras 64–105.

4.8.15

1   [*Contd*] This case law was applied in *R v North West Lancashire Health Authority, ex p A, D and G* [2000] 1 WLR 977 (Court of Appeal) to arrive at the conclusion that art 8 could not be used to found any right to gender reassignment surgery.

4.8.20

3   [*Contd*] See also *Söderbäck v Sweden* (1998) 29 EHRR 95, EComHR, para 35; E Ct HR, para 24. At para 33 the E Ct HR confirmed the competing 'family life' considerations in favour of the child's step-father who had successfully obtained a formal adoption order after six and a half years of de facto parenting.

4.8.22

1   [*Contd*] This case law has now been analysed and applied by the majority of the House of Lords in *Fitzpatrick v Sterling Housing Association* [1999] 1 WLR 1113; and by the ECJ in *Grant v South West Trains Ltd* [1998] ICR 449, 478, para 35.

4.8.25

1   See, more recently *TP and KM v United Kingdom*, 10 September 1999, EComHR, para 67.

4.8.33   [*Contd*] By contrast, the EComHR has recently taken a more restrictive view of what constitutes a 'home' in the case of *Frederick and David Barclay v United Kingdom*². The EComHR held that the mere ownership of property (there, the Channel Island of Brecqhou where the applicants' home was under construction but they were not living) is not sufficient to render it a 'home'.

1   [*Contd*] See also *R v North and East Devon Health Authority, ex p Coughlan* [2000] 2 WLR 622 (where a local authority residential facility constituted a home) and *Mentes v Turkey* (1997) 26 EHRR 595, E Ct HR, para 73 (a house occupied for significant periods on an annual basis, together with a strong family connection, constitutes a 'home'). And see similar cases noted under para **4.13.15**, n 16 below.
2   Application 35712/97 *Frederick and David Barclay v United Kingdom*, Comm Rep 18 May 1999, EComHR.

4.8.34

1   [*Contd*] See also *Camenzind v Switzerland* (1998) 28 EHRR 458, E Ct HR, para 35; *Larkos v Cyprus* (1999) 7 BHRC 244, ECtHR, paras 25–30.
3   [*Contd*] See also *Pemberton v London Borough of Southwark* (CA, unreported 13 April 2000) in which the domestic court was persuaded to develop domestic principles of nuisance in a fashion consistent with art 8 so as to hold that a 'tolerated trespasser' has standing to sue for nuisance.
4   [*Contd*] The notion of a home does not connote the physical presence of the owner/occupier: see *McLeod v United Kingdom* (1999) 27 EHRR 493, E Ct HR (entry by police into applicant's home during her absence).

4.8.35 [*Contd*] The case of *Camenzind v Switzerland* leaves open the question of whether an owner of residential property has standing to sue on behalf of his tenants where their property is searched along with his own[4].

4 *Camenzind v Switzerland* (1998) 28 EHRR 458, E Ct HR, paras 32–35.

4.8.37

1 [*Contd*] But unauthorised entry onto, and filming on, property owned by another does not, without more, necessarily entail any interference with private life; nor does the failure of domestic law to provide a pre-emptive remedy to prevent such entry: see *Frederick and David Barclay v United Kingdom*, 18 May 1999, EComHR.
5 [*Contd*] In *R v North and East Devon Health Authority, ex p Coughlan* [2000] 2 WLR 622, closure of a residential home (as to which representations had been made to the Applicant about her right to stay indefinitely) was held to constitute an interference.

4.8.38

1 [*Contd*] See also *McGinley and Egan v United Kingdom* (1998) 27 EHRR 1, E Ct HR, para 99 (access to information for ex-servicemen stationed on or near Christmas Island at the time of British nuclear tests in 1958), distinguishing *Guerra v Italy*. It was held, by five votes to four, that there was no violation.

4.8.39

3 [*Contd*] *Khan v United Kingdom* (2000) Times, 23 May, E Ct HR, para 25 (transcript recorded by a listening device, fitted by police in premises used by a suspected drug trafficker, later used at trial).
4 [*Contd*] *Govell v United Kingdom*, EComHR, (14 January 1998, unreported). *Valenzuela Contreras v Spain* (1998) 28 EHRR 483, E Ct HR, para 47, shows that the practice of 'metering' is an 'interference' as well as the recording of conversations, albeit one with potentially less far-reaching impact.
5 [*Contd*] *Foxley v United Kingdom* (2000) Times, 4 July, E Ct HR (interference with a bankrupt's correspondence *after* the expiry of a valid court order redirecting his mail to his trustee in bankruptcy was held to be a reach of the right to respect for corresponding because it was not 'in accordance with law': moreover, the opening, reading and copying *before* the expiry of the order of the bankrupt's correspondence with his lawyer was also a breach of the same right because it was not 'necessary in a democratic society' to interfere with such an important confidential and privileged relationship.
6 [*Contd*] A number of domestic cases have considered the applicability of art 8 to the use of registers of criminal convictions or even allegations of criminal conduct (particularly those entailing sexual offences) and/or the disclosure of information as to such convictions/allegations: see *R v Chief Constable of North Wales, ex p Thorpe* [1999] QB 396, CA; *Woolgar v Chief Constable of the Sussex Police* [1999] 3 All ER 604, CA; *R v Local Authority and Police Authority in the Midlands, ex p LM* [2000] UKHRR 143.

4.8.43

3 [*Contd*] *Valenzuela Contreras v Spain* (1998) 28 EHRR 483, E Ct HR.
5 [*Contd*] *McLeod v United Kingdom* (1998) 27 EHRR 493, E Ct HR (entry by police into applicant's home held not to be proportionate to the legitimate aim of preventing disorder and crime).

4.8.45

3 [*Contd*] For a description of the E Ct HR's recent examination of the Ministry of Defence's policy that homosexuality was, in itself, incompatible with service in the armed forces, see para **4.8.13A** above and *Smith and Grady v United Kingdom* (1999) 29 EHRR 493 and *Lustig-Prean and Beckett v United Kingdom* (1999) 29 EHRR 548. For a brief domestic analysis of the justification and proportionality of a decision (under arts 8 and 10) to lift reporting restrictions in a case involving a minor see *R v Teesdale and Wear Valley Justices, ex p M* (Div Ct, 7 February 2000, unreported).

4.8.46 [*Contd*] The forcible examination of a mentally handicapped person in hospital, the deprivation of whose legal capacity must be regularly reviewed, may be justified in the interests of that patient's own rights and health (especially when ample opportunity for consent to the examination has been given)[5].

5   *Matter v Slovakia*, judgment 5 July 1999, E Ct HR, paras 65–72.

4.8.47

2   [*Contd*] The approach in *Johansen* was distinguished in *Söderbäck v Sweden* (1998) 29 EHRR 95 where the E Ct HR, paras 30–31, departed from the approach of the EComHR to apply a less strict proportionality test. The main reasons for this approach were, first, the competing claims of the natural father and of the adoptive father to 'family life' with the child (as opposed to the child being taken into care), paras 32–33, and, second, the better position of the national authorities to evaluate the strength of these competing claims and thus to determine a 'fair balance' between them, para 33. For these reasons, the decision of the Swedish courts to permit the formal adoption of the child, against her natural father's wishes, fell within the margin of appreciation.

4.8.48

1   [*Contd*] See also *TP and KM v United Kingdom*, 10 September 1999, EComHR, paras 68–77 (failure to provide a parent with a proper, fair or adequate opportunity promptly to participate in the decision-making procedures after the emergency removal of a child from the family home violates the rights of both parent and child) and *K and T v Finland*, 27 April 2000, E Ct HR, paras 131–176 (art 8 violated by the taking into care of a child and the restriction and prohibition of rights of parental access).
4   [*Contd*] See also *Söderbäck v Sweden* (1998) 29 EHRR 95, E Ct HR.

4.8.51   [*Contd*] Similarly, in *McLeod v United Kingdom*[5] the E Ct HR had to

consider the entry by the police into the applicant's home in support of her former husband's removal of matrimonial chattels. The entry was held to be 'in accordance with the law' because the power of the police to enter private premises without a warrant in order to deal with or prevent a breach of the peace was legitimate and precisely defined. However, in the ECtHR the entry was held to be disproportionate to the legitimate aim pursued (the prevention of disorder and crime) because the police did not take any steps to check that the applicant's former husband was entitled to enter the premises under a court order or that the applicant (who was not present) had agreed that he should do so.

5   (1998) 27 EHRR 493, E Ct HR, paras 52–58.

4.8.52

1   [*Contd*] See also *Camenzind v Switzerland* (1998) 28 EHRR 458, E Ct HR, paras 41–47, where a search conducted to obtain evidence of a relatively minor offence was found to be proportionate because of its limited ambit and sensible implementation. The E Ct HR did, however, stress at para 45 that particular vigilance was required where a search was permitted without a judicial warrant. In *Wilson v Lane* (1999) 7 BHRC 274 the US SC condemned as unjustifiable and unconstitutional the practice of allowing journalists to 'tailgate' the police in their execution of search warrants.

4.8.53

3   [*Contd*] The phrase in art 8(2) 'in accordance with the law' not only requires compliance with domestic law but also relates to the quality of that law, requiring it to be compatible with the rule of law. In the context of covert surveillance, domestic law must provide protection against arbitrary interference with an individual's rights under art 8. It must also be sufficiently clear, and measures taken under it sufficiently foreseeable, to give individuals an adequate indication of the circumstances in which and the conditions on which public authorities are entitled to use covert measures. In *Khan v United Kingdom* (2000) Times, 23 May, the E Ct HR, paras 26–28, found a

violation on precisely this ground (aural surveillance not 'in accordance with the law' because the Home Office Guidelines, although complied with, were neither legally binding nor publicly accessible); following *Govell v United Kingdom*, 14 January 1998, EComHR, paras 61–62. See now the Police Act 1997 which provides a statutory framework for covert surveillance. The E Ct HR also stressed the seriousness of the interference with private life and correspondence constituted by surveillance in *Kopp v Switzerland* (1998) 27 EHRR 91, paras 63–76 (where it concluded that the rules governing the tapping of lawyers' telephone lines were insufficiently clear). See similarly *Amman v Switzerland*, E Ct HR, (16 February 2000, unreported).

4 [*Contd*] *Valenzuela Contreras v Spain* (1998) 28 EHRR 483, E Ct HR, paras 46 and 50–61. A violation was found because the Spanish telephone tapping regime did not specify, in binding legal codes or judgments, precisely when the power to tap could be exercised. As such, the application of the tapping regime was not sufficiently foreseeable to be 'in accordance with law'.

4.8.54

1 [*Contd*] This case law was applied by the Divisional Court in *R v Chesterfield Justices, ex p Bramley* [2000] 1 All ER 411.

4.8.56 [*Contd*] In *MS v Sweden*[3] the Court held that disclosure by a state-run medical clinic to the state social security body of confidential information contained in medical records (without prior warning to the applicant/patient) could be justified as having pursued the legitimate aim of 'protecting the economic well being of the country' and as being 'necessary in a democratic society'. The applicant injured her back at work and claimed state compensation. The claim had to be assessed and there was a legitimate need to check it against the medical information. The E Ct HR held that the communication, for this purpose, of the medical records held at the clinic where the applicant sought treatment was potentially decisive for the allocation of public funds to deserving claimants. The E Ct HR was also reassured by the existence of effective and adequate safeguards against abuse. The information was kept by the social security body upon the same terms and conditions as it was by the state clinic. Staff in both bodies could incur civil and/or criminal liability if they failed to observe those terms and conditions. *MS v Sweden* was applied by the Divisional Court in *R v Secretary of State for the Home Department, ex p Kingdom of Belgium*[4]. See also in this respect *General Mediterranean Holdings SA v Patel*[5] where disclosure of legally privileged materials for a wasted costs application was refused because it would have infringed art 8. The interests being protected by a wasted costs application were held to be insufficient to justify interference with such an important right.

1 [*Contd*] See also the proportionality analysis in *R v Chief Constable of North Wales, ex p Thorpe* [1999] QB 396, CA; *Woolgar v Chief Constable of the Sussex Police* [1999] 3 All ER 604, CA and *R v A Local Authority and Police Authority in the Midlands, ex p LM* [2000] UKHRR 143.
3 (1998) 28 EHRR 313, E Ct HR, paras 38–44.
4 (15 February 2000, unreported).
5 [2000] 1 WLR 272.

Article 9 Freedom of thought, conscience and religion

4.9.6 [*Contd*] The HRA 1998 does not define the term 'religion' in art 9 of the Convention, or in s 13(1) of the HRA 1998[3]. The interpretation given by the UN Human Rights Committee to art 18 of the ICCPR[4], which is the equivalent of art 9 of the Convention, is of assistance on the issue of definition. In its General Comment 22 (1993), para 2, the Human Rights Committee explained that art 18:

'protects theistic, non-theistic and atheistic beliefs as well as the right not to profess any religion or belief. The terms belief and religion are broadly construed. Article 18 is not limited in its application to traditional religions or practices analogous to those of traditional religions. The Committee therefore views with concern any tendency to discriminate against any religion or belief for any reason, including the fact that they are newly established, or represent religious minorities that may be the subject of hostility by a predominant religious community.'

3 See para **2.13.1** above.
4 See para **8.10** below.

4.9.7 [*Contd*] In its General Comment 22, para 9, the Human Rights Committee observed, in the context of art 18 and art 26 (right to equal protection without discrimination), that measures discriminating against adherents of minority religions or non-believers are 'not in accordance with the prohibition of non-discrimination based on religion or belief and the guarantee of equal protection under Article 26'. The strict theistic approach to the definition of religion under English law is likely to be too restrictive for the purposes of the Convention[10] and will lead to discrimination against newer faiths and non-theistic belief systems. The approach adopted by the High Court of Australia in *Church of the New Faith v Comr For Pay-Roll Tax*[12] is likely to be of greater assistance to the English Courts than the older English authorities in developing an autonomous Convention definition of religion, which will avoid such discriminatory results and will include the full range of traditional and modern systems of belief within a core definition. As Mason ACJ and Brennan J explained in their joint judgment[13] in Church of the New Faith case:

'Freedom of religion, the paradigm freedom of conscience, is the essence of a free society. The chief function in the law of a definition of religion is to mark out an area within which a person subject to the law is free to believe and to act in accordance with his belief without legal restraint. Such a definition affects the scope and operation of s 116 of the Constitution and identifies the subject matters which other laws are presumed not to affect. Religion is thus a concept of fundamental importance to the law'.

10 As to this approach see *R v Registrar General, ex Segerdal* [1970] 2 QB 697, CA and *Re South Place Ethical Society* [1980] 1 WLR 1565, Ch D. See also Quint and Spring,'Religion, Charity Law and Human Rights', Charity Law and Practice Review 5 (1999) 153.
11 (1982) 154 CLR 120 (High Court of Australia). The approach adopted by the High Court of Australia has been endorsed and applied without qualification in the High Court of New Zealand: *Centrepoint Community Growth Trust v IRC* [1985] 1 NZLR 673 (Tompkins J). As to the approach to definition

taken in other common law jurisdictions see: *The Commissioner, Hindu Religious Endowments, Madras v Sri Lakshmiranda Thirtha Swamiar of Sri Shirur Mutt* [1954] SCR 1005 (SC of India); *Ratilal Panachand Gandhi v State of Bombay* AIR 1954 SC 388; *Mittal v Union of India* AIR 1983 SC 1 (SC of India); *In Re Chikweche* 1995 (4) SA 284 (ZC) (SC of Zimbabwe); *Torcasco v Watkins* 367 US 488 (1961) (US SC); *Malnak v Yogi* 592 F 2d 197 (1979) (US Court of Appeals, Third Circuit); *US v Sun Myung Moon* 718 F 2d 1210 (1983) (US Court of Appeals, Second Circuit); and *Church of Scientology Flag Service Org Inc v City of Clearwater* 2 F 3d 1514 (1993) (US Court of Appeals, Eleventh Circuit). See also para **2.13.1**, n 2.

12   (1982) 154 CLR 120 (High Court of Australia) at 130.

4.10

Article 10 Freedom of expression

4.10.2A In *R v Secretary of State for the Home Department, ex p Simms*[1], Lord Steyn relied upon art 10 of the Convention, as reflected in the common law, in holding that the Secretary of State's policy of refusing to permit prisoners to have interviews with journalists to discuss their claims of miscarriages of justice was ultra vires as an unjustifiable interference with prisoners' rights of freedom of expression at common law. Lord Steyn explained[2]:

> 'freedom of speech is the lifeblood of democracy. The free flow of information and ideas informs political debate. It is a safety valve: people are more ready to accept decisions that go against them if they can in principle seek to influence them. It acts as a brake on the abuse of power by public officials. It facilitates the exposure of errors in the governance and administration of justice in the country'.

1   [1999] 3 WLR 328, HL.
2   At 337B–C. See also *Reynolds v Times Newspapers Ltd* [1999] 3 WLR 1010, HL: see para **1.79** above.

4.10.2B English law recognises a defence of qualified privilege[1] in circumstances not necessarily limited to political speech. Lord Nicholls, for the majority in *Reynolds*[2], provided a non-exhaustive list of matters which the Court should take into account when considering whether a factually inaccurate publication should benefit from this defence. These matters include: the nature of the information and the extent to which the subject-matter is a matter of public interest; the seriousness of the allegations; the source of the information; the steps taken to verify the information; whether the allegation has been the source of an investigation which commands respect; the urgency of matter; and whether the claimant's side of the story has been given. Lord Nicholls considered the Convention jurisprudence (see para **4.10.14** below) and held that this approach accorded with such case-law, particularly its emphasis on the need for accuracy on matters of fact in contrast to the wider freedom to publish value-judgments not susceptible to proof.

1   *Reynolds v Times Newspapers Ltd* [1999] 3 WLR 1010, HL. The same panel of Law Lords, sitting as the Judicial Committee of the Privy Council, allowed the appeal of Mr Lange from the New Zealand Court of Appeal in *Lange v Atkinson and Australian Consolidated Press NZ Ltd* [1997] 2 NZLR 22 (New Zealand Court of Appeal), and remitted the matter back to the New Zealand Court of Appeal to decide whether local social and political conditions in New Zealand required the common law in that jurisdiction to follow a different course from that declared in *Reynolds*. The New Zealand Court of Appeal in its judgment of 21 June 2000 (unreported) decided not to depart from its earlier judgment and affirmed the existence of a general defence of qualified privilege applying to political statements published by the media. It held that the *Reynolds* decision altered the law of qualified privilege in a way which added to the uncertainty and chilling effect of the existing law of libel. The Court also observed that the decision in *Reynolds* confused the distinct concepts of occasion of privilege and abuse of privilege by allowing factors relevant to abuse of privilege to determine whether the occasion was one of privilege.
2   At 1027C–F.

4.10.3A In *Wille v Liechtenstein*[1], the applicant, President of the Liechtenstein

Administrative Court, gave an academic lecture concerning the competence of the Constitutional Court and stated his opinion that the Constitutional Court had jurisdiction to rule on disputes concerning the powers of the monarch, the Prince. The applicant, prior to his appointment, had been involved in such a dispute with the Prince as a member of a previous government. In response to the lecture, the Prince wrote a private letter to the applicant stating his displeasure with the applicant and his intention not to appoint the applicant to public office again. The E Ct HR held that the applicant's status as a civil servant did not deprive him of the protection of art 10, and that the Prince's letter constituted an interference with the right to freedom of expression. It further held that even allowing for a certain margin of appreciation, the Prince's action was disproportionate to any legitimate aim since the issue considered at the lecture was a matter of genuine academic debate and no instance was put before the E Ct HR of the applicant, in the course of his judicial duties or otherwise, having acted in an objectionable manner, or having allowed his personal views to have any bearing on his performance as President of the Administrative Court.

1   (28 October 1999, unreported) E Ct HR.

4.10.3B   In *Steel v United Kingdom*[1], the applicants complained that orders that they agree to be bound over to keep the peace were an uncertain and disproportionate restriction on their rights under art 10 and art 11 of the Convention. The Government sought to argue that the applicants did not enjoy rights under these provisions since they were not involved in peaceful activities at the time of their arrest. The E Ct HR accepted that the applicants had been seeking to impede a grouse shoot and motorway extension, respectively, but concluded that they were nevertheless engaged in acts of protected expression within art 10. The E Ct HR also held that the interference with certain of the applicants' rights under art 10 were not 'prescribed by law' on the basis that they had been arrested and detained in circumstances where art 5(1) had been violated.

1   (1998) 28 EHRR 603, E Ct HR.

4.10.6   In *Fuentes Bobo v Spain*[1], the applicant, a television producer employed by a Spanish television station, was dismissed from his employment following disparaging and offensive comments, including value-judgments, made by him on radio programmes concerning the way in which the television station was managed and operated. The E Ct HR held that the sanction imposed on the applicant was a disproportionate interference with the applicant's rights under article 10 given the circumstances in which the broadcast was made, the applicant's length of service, the applicant's age and the alternative sanctions available. The E Ct HR emphasised that the applicant had made his comments on the radio station as part of a fast moving debate on a matter of public concern and that although he had used intemperate language his statements had been made in response to rapid and provocative questioning by the radio interviewer. The Spanish Government sought to argue that the television station was a private commercial entity subject in its relations with the applicant to private law employment legislation, rather than part of the administration of the state. The E Ct HR rejected this submission and held that although the applicant was disciplined in the context of a private law employment relationship, the applicant's art 10 rights were interfered with because the overriding context in which he made his comments went beyond the immediate private sphere and concerned a subject of vigorous national debate, namely the running of the public television service. This aspect of the decision of the E Ct HR is important in the protection it affords to the right to freedom of expression as between purely private persons in a contractual relationship. The logic of the E Ct HR's reasoning is that where the subject-matter of the expression of views is in fact one of national concern, the State is obliged to ensure that a private employer does not unnecessarily restrict such expression, thereby giving a certain degree of horizontal effect to the Convention. See generally para **2.6.3** above. In *R v Secretary of State for Health, ex p Wagstaff*[2], the Divisional Court held that the decision of the Secretary of State directing that the inquiry into the Dr Harold Shipman affair should take evidence in private was irrational. Kennedy LJ, for the Court, explained that the decision was a disproportionate interference with the rights of Shipman's victims' families to receive information from those giving evidence. The Divisional Court held further that the Secretary of State had not shown the need to have the inquiry in private and restated the principle that even prior to the coming into force of the Human Rights Act 1998, freedom of expression is recognised by the common law as a fundamental human right which can only lawfully be restricted to the extent required to meet a pressing social need.

1   (29 February 2000, unreported) E Ct HR.
2   (20 July 2000, unreported) Divisional Court.

4.10.12A   In a series of related cases[1] arising out of criminal proceedings taken against the owner of a newspaper for publishing press articles, readers' letters and reports concerning the conflict between the Turkish Government and the Kurds, the E Ct HR has emphasised that there is little scope under art 10(2) of the Convention for press restrictions on political speech or on debate on questions of public interest. The E Ct HR observed that in a democratic system the actions and omissions of the government must be subject to the close scrutiny not only of the legislative and judicial authorities but also of public opinion, and that the government was required to display particular restraint in resorting to criminal proceedings in this context. In each of these cases, the E Ct HR itself analysed the nature and content of the impugned publications, in light of the situation of tension and conflict in Turkey, in deciding whether the interference with the applicants' rights was justified and proportionate. In *Surek and Ozdemir v Turkey*[1], the E Ct HR found the interference to be disproportionate where the relevant publications, interviews with leaders of prohibited parties, did not incite violence and simply sought to communicate the views of the opposition. The E Ct HR came to the same conclusion in *Surek v Turkey (No 4)*[1] which concerned a news commentary describing the Kurdish cause as well as interviews with the opposition. In *Surek v Turkey (No 1)*[1], however, the E Ct HR found the applicant's conviction for publishing letters which sought to incite violence to be justified under art 10(2). Similarly in *Surek v Turkey (No 3)*[1], the E Ct HR found that a conviction based on the publication of a news commentary which provided the writer with an outlet for stirring up violence was proportionate to a legitimate aim. In *Surek v Turkey (No 2)*[1], the E Ct HR held that prosecution of a journalist for publishing the names of police and gendarme officers who had been implicated in serious misconduct served the legitimate purpose of seeking to prevent the officers from terrorist attack, but because their names were already in the public domain, the interference was disproportionate to the legitimate aim. The E Ct HR relied upon the Spycatcher[2] cases in holding that where there had already been prior disclosure, the potential damage which the restriction was aimed at preventing had already been done and therefore served no useful purpose. In each of these cases, the E Ct HR rejected the submission of the owner of the newspaper that since he had only a commercial rather than an editorial relationship with the publications, he was to be exonerated from any criminal liability for the contents of the publications[3]. The E Ct HR explained that the owner was 'vicariously subject to the "duties and responsibilities" which the review's editorial and journalist staff undertake in the collection and dissemination of information to the public and which assume an even greater importance in situations of conflict and tension'[4].

1   *Surek and Ozdemir v Turkey* (8 July 1999, unreported) *Surek v Turkey (No1)* (8 July 1999, unreported) E Ct HR; *Surek v Turkey (No 3)* (8 July 1999, unreported) E Ct HR; *Surek v Turkey (No 4)* (8 July 1999, unreported) E Ct HR; and *Surek v Turkey (No 4)*, July 1999, E Ct HR. See also *Arslan v Turkey* (8 July 1999, unreported) E Ct HR (publication of a book), *Gerger v Turkey*, 8 July 1999, E Ct HR (letter read out at a meeting), *Karatas v Turkey* (8 July 1999, unreported) E Ct HR (poetry), *Okcuoglu v Turkey* (8 July 1999, unreported) E Ct HR (periodical containing record of speech at a round-table conference), and *Ceylan v Turkey* (8 July 1999, unreported) (article by union leader on the Kurdish problem), in each of which the E Ct HR found violations of art 10 in respect of criminal prosecutions of the applicants who had written material which was critical of the Turkish Government and supportive of the Kurdish cause. In *Ozgur Gundem v Turkey* (16 March 2000, unreported) E Ct HR, the Court held Turkey had failed to take adequate protective and investigative measures to protect the applicant newspaper's exercise of its freedom of expression and that it had imposed measures on the newspaper, through search and arrest operations and through numerous prosecutions and convictions in respect of issues of the newspaper, which were disproportionate and unjustified in the pursuit of any legitimate aim. As a result of these cumulative factors, the newspaper ceased publication and the Court found a breach of art 10 of the Convention.
2   *Sunday Times Ltd v United Kingdom (No 2)* (1991) 14 EHRR 229, E Ct HR and *Observer and Guardian v United Kingdom* (1991) 14 EHRR 153, E Ct HR.
3   The E Ct HR has also rejected the submission that a publisher and distributor do not (in contrast to a writer) enjoy the right to freedom of expression by holding that publishers and distributors enjoy the right by providing authors with an essential medium of communication: see *Ozturk v Turkey* (28 September 1999, unreported) E Ct HR, para 49.
4   *Surek v Turkey (No 2)* (8 July 1999, unreported) E Ct HR, para 36.

4.10.12B   The Supreme Court of Zimbabwe in *Chavunduka v Minister of Home Affairs*[1], struck down as unconstitutional the provisions of legislation which made it an offence to publish false statements which were 'likely to cause fear, alarm or despondency among the public'. The Claimants were newspaper journalists who had been prosecuted under these provisions for publishing an article reporting a failed coup attempt by senior army officers. Gubbay CJ, giving the leading judgment, canvassed a wide range of common law freedom of expression authorities, relying in particular upon the jurisprudence of the E Ct HR and the United States and Canadian Supreme Courts. The Supreme Court of Zimbabwe held that the provisions in question were vague and overbroad and likely to exert an unacceptable 'chilling effect' on freedom of expression. Accordingly, the provisions did not satisfy the test of being 'under the authority of any law' when that phrase was interpreted in accordance with the meaning given by the E Ct HR to the equivalent words 'prescribed by law' in *The Sunday Times v United Kingdom*[2]. The Supreme Court further held that the respondent had not discharged the burden of establishing that the objective of the legislation was a 'pressing and substantial concern' in a democratic society, the analogue of the test of 'pressing social need'[3] in the jurisprudence of the E Ct HR. In *R v Central Criminal Court, ex p The Guardian*[4], the Divisional Court allowed, in part, an appeal against orders requiring newspapers and journalists to disclose materials relating to contacts they had made with the ex MI6 agent, David Shayler. Judge LJ, for the Court, explained that the original orders would have a devastating and stifling effect on the proper investigation of the Shayler story and that this was disproportionate to any practical advantage to the prosecution process. Citing Lord Steyn's speech in *Simms* (see para **4.10.2A**), Judge LJ observed:

'Inconvenient or embarrassing revelations, whether for the security services or for public authorities, should not be suppressed. Legal proceedings directed towards the seizure of the working papers of individual journalists, or the premises of the newspaper or television programme publishing his or her report, or the threat of such proceedings tends to inhibit discussion. When a genuine investigation into possible corrupt or reprehensible activities by a public authority is being investigated by the media, compelling evidence would normally be needed to demonstrate that the public interest will be served by such proceedings. Otherwise, to the public's disadvantage, legitimate enquiry and discussion and "the safety valve of effective investigative journalism" ... would be discouraged, perhaps stifled.'

1   (22 May 2000, unreported).
2   (1979) 2 EHRR 245 at 271, E Ct HR. See para **3.13** above.
3   See para **3.15** above.
4   (21 July 2000, unreported), Divisional Court.

4.10.12C   In *Rekvényi v Hungary*[1], the applicant, a police officer and Secretary General of the Police Independent Trade Union, challenged a provision of the Constitution of Hungary which prevented members of the armed forces, the police and security services from joining any political party or engaging in political activity. The E Ct HR found that the restriction pursued the legitimate aim of protection of national security and the prevention of disorder in circumstances where the restriction was introduced at a time when Hungary was seeking to depoliticise the police during its transformation from a totalitarian regime to a pluralist democracy. Relying upon *Ahmed v United Kingdom*[2], the E Ct HR explained that the public were entitled to expect that in their dealings with the police they would be confronted with politically-neutral officers who were detached from the political fray. By reason of the particular historical background in which the restriction had been introduced and because of the fact that under the domestic legislation police officers were still entitled to undertake certain political activities, as opposed to being subject to an absolute ban, the Court held that the interference was justified within art 10(2). The constitutional legality of restrictions of free speech rights of the armed force was considered in *South African National Defence Union v Minister of Defence*[3]. The South African Constitutional Court held that provisions of the Defence Act 1957 which prevented members of the defence force from participating in acts of 'public protest' and from joining a trade union[4] were overbroad and unconstitutional. O'Regan J, for the Court, explained:

'The scope of the provision under challenge suggests that members of the defence force are not entitled to form, air and hear opinions on matters of public concern. It suggests that enrolment in the defence force requires a detachment from the interests and activities of ordinary society and of ordinary citizens. Such a conception of a defence force cannot be correct. Members of the defence force remain part of our society, with obligations and rights of citizenship'.

1   (1999) 6 BHRC 554, E Ct HR.
2   (1998) 5 BHRC 111 , E Ct HR: see para **4.10.14**.
3   (1999) 6 BHRC 574, Const Court of South Africa.

4 See para **4.11.6**.

4.10.14 [*Contd*] In *Bladet Tromso v Norway*[8], the E Ct HR held that the defamation proceedings brought against the applicant newspaper and its editor in respect of the publication of an article concerning the seal-hunting industry were not a proportionate measure under art 10(2) for the purpose of protecting the reputation of crew members of the ship named in the article. The E Ct HR proceeded on the basis that the newspaper was ordinarily under an obligation to verify the factual accuracy of a statement defamatory of private individuals unless there were special grounds not to do so in the present case[9]. The E Ct HR found such special circumstances on the facts relying, in particular, upon the following matters: the fact that the impugned articles were part of an ongoing debate on an issue of local, national and international concern in which the views of a wide selection of persons were reported; that the newspaper had repeated allegations made in a government inspector's report which had only later been rejected by an inquiry; that the allegations were not made against any specific crew members but the crew as a whole; and that the newspaper had acted in good faith in relying upon the inspector's conclusions. As to publications on matters of public interest, see also *Bergens Tiende v Norway*[10] where the Court found that defamation proceedings against a newspaper which had published reports concerning cosmetic surgery carried out by a doctor were a disproportionate interference with the applicant newspaper's art 10 rights by reason of the fact that the matter printed was broadly factually accurate and the fact that the issue of medical care was one of public concern and the subject of debate within the community. In *Dalban v Romania*[11], the E Ct HR found that the conviction of the applicant journalist of criminal libel in circumstances where he had published an article accusing a member of the board of representatives for a State farm of fraud was a disproportionate interference with the applicant's rights. The E Ct HR relied, in particular, upon the fact that there was no proof that the facts alleged were untrue (the domestic courts having ignored the applicant's evidence that the facts were true) and that the article had been limited to a discussion of the representative's behaviour and capacity as an elected representative rather than about his private life. In *Wabl v Austria*[12], the E Ct HR found that an injunction restraining the applicant politician from repeating the expression 'Nazi-journalism' in relation to a newspaper which had defamed him by suggesting he was suffering from AIDS was necessary in a democratic society for the protection of the reputation of the newspaper. The Court emphasised that the reproach came close to a charge of criminal behaviour by the newspaper and that the injunction was limited in its terms such as not to prevent the applicant from voicing his opinion, using other language, concerning the newspaper.

8 (2000) 29 EHRR 125, E Ct HR.
9 This is also the approach adopted by the common law of qualified privilege: see para **4.10.2.B** above.
10 (2 May 2000, unreported) E Ct HR. See also *Nilsen and Johnsen v Norway* (25 November 1999, unreported) E Ct HR, where the Court held that the applicants, elected representatives of professional police associations, had not exceeded the acceptable limits of permissible criticism when making defamatory comments, in the form of value-judgments rather than statements of fact, concerning the author of publications making allegations of police violence. The E Ct HR found however, in one respect, where an allegation of deliberate lies had been made, the applicants had exceeded such limits since this was an allegation of fact which the applicants should be required to prove.
11 (28 September 1999, unreported) E Ct HR.
12 (21 March 2000, unreported) E Ct HR.

4.10.15   [*Contd*] In *Sir Elton John v Express Newspapers plc*[2], the Court of Appeal held that disclosure of the source of a confidential draft legal opinion which had been taken from a barristers' chambers and supplied to a national newspaper had not been shown to be necessary on the facts of the case. The Court of Appeal emphasised that where orders were to be made requiring journalists to depart from their normal professional standards of confidentiality, the merits of their doing so in the public interest must be clearly demonstrated. On the facts, the chambers had made no attempt to conduct an internal investigation to find the culprit prior to applying to the Court and this factor defeated any submission that disclosure by the journalist was necessary in the interests of justice.

2   [2000] 3 All ER 257, CA.

4.11

Article 11 Right to freedom of peaceful assembly and association

4.11.2 [*Contd*] The House of Lords has held, by a majority, that at common law the public have the right to use a highway for peaceful assembly in a manner consistent with the primary right to use it for passage and repassage[10]. Accordingly, a peaceful assembly for a reasonable period that does not unreasonably obstruct the highway is lawful. Lord Irvine of Lairg LC stated in *DPP v Jones* that if the common law of trespass was not clear in providing for such a result, then having regard to art 11 of the Convention, it should be declared to allow such peaceful assemblies. He explained at 259E–F that:

> 'Unless the common law recognises that assembly on the public highway may be lawful, the right contained in article 11(1) of the Convention is denied. Of course the right may be subject to restrictions. But in my judgment our law will not comply with the Convention unless its starting-point is that assembly on the highway will not necessarily be unlawful. I reject an approach which entails that such an assembly will always be tortious and therefore unlawful.'

Lord Hutton[11] also held that the common law should recognise a right of assembly on the highway and that the following reasoning of the Supreme Court of Canada in *Committee for the Commonwealth of Canada v Canada*[12] should also apply in declaring the scope of the common law right of public assembly:

> 'freedom of expression cannot be exercised in a vacuum... it necessarily implies the use of physical space in order to meet its underlying objectives. No one could agree that the exercise of freedom of expression can be limited solely to places owned by the person wishing to communicate: such an approach would certainly deny the very foundation of the freedom of expression.'

10 *DPP v Jones* [1999] 2 AC 240, HL.
11 At 288G.
12 (1991) 77 DLR (4th) 385 (SC of Canada) at 394.

4.11.6 [*Contd*] The South African Constitutional Court held in *South African National Defence Union v Minister of Defence*[4] that members of the defence forces fall within the definition of 'workers' under s 23 of the Constitution of the Republic of South Africa and accordingly enjoy the right to form and join trade unions. Provisions of a domestic statute which prohibited such persons from joining trade unions were therefore declared unconstitutional. In interpreting the term 'workers', the Constitutional Court of South Africa had regard to[5] the Freedom of Association and Protection of the Right to Organise Convention (San Francisco, 9 July 1948, ILO Convention no 87 of 1948), and the Right to Organise and Collective Bargaining Convention (Geneva, 1 July 1949, ILO Convention no 98 of 1949), which had been ratified by South Africa and which recognised that, subject to regulation in national law, the members of the armed forces and the police were workers for the purposes of the Conventions and had the right to organise. The Court held that given that members of the armed forces had a constitutional right to organise, a blanket ban on joining trade unions went beyond what was reasonable and justifiable to achieve the legitimate objective of maintaining a disciplined military force. O'Regan J[6], for the Court, considered the comparative position in England, France, and the United States where no trade unions are permitted in the armed forces, but distinguished the position in those countries on the basis that none of these countries provided an express constitutional right to form and join trade unions. However, on considering the wording of art 11(2), it can be argued that the members of the armed forces do in fact enjoy such a constitutional right, subject to regulation or restriction; a position which is identical to the right declared to exist by the South African Constitutional Court. In these circumstances, the legality under the Convention of a blanket ban on trade union membership and activity by the armed forces, as opposed to regulation of that right where justified and proportionate, is open to doubt.

4   (1999) 6 BHRC 574 (Const Court of South Africa).
5   Section 39 of the Constitution of the Republic of South Africa provides that when a court is interpreting Ch 2 of the Constitution it must consider international law.
6   586c–f.

4.12

Article 12 Right to marry and found a family

4.12.10

2   [*Contd*] See also Case C-249/96: *Grant v South-West Trains* [1998] ECR I-621, ECJ at paras 34–35, referring to *Rees and Cossey* and concluding that in EC law too 'stable relationships between two persons of the same sex are not regarded as equivalent to marriages or stable relationships outside marriage between persons of the opposite sex'.

4.13
Article 13 Right to an effective remedy

4.13.1

1   [*Contd*] Because the requirements of art 13 are less strict than those of other parts of the Convention, the E Ct HR frequently states that art 13's requirements are absorbed by those of other articles. Thus, once it has found a breach of another article, the E Ct HR very often concludes that no separate issue arises under art 13. *Osman v United Kingdom* (1998) 29 EHRR 245, paras 157–158, E Ct HR and *Tinnelly & Son Ltd and McElduff v United Kingdom* (1999) 27 EHRR 249, para 87, E Ct HR are recent examples (both involving art 6). Conversely, when a complaint based upon other articles fails, the E Ct HR is prone to saying that a complaint based upon the 'less strict' terms of art 13 is thereby bound to fail: *Hood v United Kingdom* (1999) Times, 11 March, paras 70–72, E Ct HR. See also *Z v United Kingdom* (1999) 28 EHRR CD65, para 121, EcomHR.

4.13.6

1   In *Wille v Liechtenstein* (28 October 1999, unreported), paras 75–78, E Ct HR, the applicant was a former President of the Liechtenstein Administrative Court. In a series of lectures he expressed opinions on constitutional law that led to criticism by the Prince in a private letter. When the Prince then decided not to re-appoint the applicant, there was no procedure by which he could challenge the dismissal. The E Ct HR found a breach of art 13 (as well as a breach of art 10 (see para **4.10.3A**)).

3   See also *Khan v United Kingdom* (2000) Times, 23 May, paras 45–47, E Ct HR.

4.13.7

7   In *Smith and Grady v United Kingdom* (1999) 29 EHRR 493, para 135, the Court summarised this case law as follows:

> '... Article 13 guarantees the availability of a remedy at a national level to enforce the substance of Convention rights and freedoms in whatever form they may happen to be secured in the domestic legal order. Thus, its effect is to require the provision of a domestic remedy allowing the competent national authority both to deal with the substance of the relevant Convention complaint and to grant appropriate relief. However, Article 13 does not go so far as to require incorporation of the Convention or a particular form of remedy, Contracting States being afforded a margin of appreciation in conforming with their obligations under this provision.'

See also *Khan v United Kingdom* (2000) Times, 23 May, para 44, E Ct HR.

4.13.10

1   [*Contd*] In *Khan v United Kingdom* (2000) Times, 23 May, para 44, the E Ct HR noted that UK criminal courts offered no effective remedy for a complaint of interference with art 8 rights by police bugging. Since the court's power under s 78 of PACE to exclude evidence did not allow those criminal courts to address the substance of the Convention complaint, namely that the bugging was other than 'in accordance with law', nor did it allow those courts to grant relief for such a finding, there was no effective remedy for a complaint alleging breach of art 8.

4.13.11

1   [*Contd*] *R v Secretary of State for the Home Department, ex p Ahmed and Patel* is now reported as *Ahmed, Patel Sosanya, Olusanya, Ibitola, Gbadegesin, Ghous, Coward, Adebayo v Secretary of State for the Home Department* [1999] Imm AR 22, CA.

4.13.12 [*Contd*] The effectiveness of judicial review proceedings for the purposes of art 13 has recently been comprehensively re-appraised by the E Ct HR in *Smith and Grady v United Kingdom*[10]. The case concerned the legality of a policy that homosexuality was, in itself, incompatible with service in the armed forces. The E Ct HR emphasised that art 13 guarantees the availability of a remedy at national level to enforce the substance of Convention rights and freedoms in whatever form they may happen to be secured in the domestic legal order. It requires that the domestic authority should be competent to deal with the substance of the relevant Convention complaint and to grant appropriate relief[11]. Domestic law and practice do not need to ensure any particular form of remedy, nor does art 13 depend on the certainty of a favourable outcome for the applicant[12]. The E Ct HR then acknowledged that the domestic test of irrationality was a high one – even allowing for the human rights context[13] – and noted that it had led to the dismissal of the judicial review application despite the sympathy which the domestic courts appeared to have for the applicants' arguments[14]. It concluded that the test 'was placed so high that it effectively excluded any consideration by the domestic courts of the question of whether [under art 8(2)] the interference with the applicants' rights answered a pressing social need or was proportionate to the national security and public order aims pursued' by the Ministry of Defence[15]. There was, therefore, no effective domestic remedy permitting the ventilation of the applicants' complaint that their right to private life had been infringed. *Vilvarajah v United Kingdom* and *Soering v United Kingdom* were distinguished on the basis that the test there applied by the domestic courts, in considering judicial review challenges to extradition and expulsion decisions, coincided with the E Ct HR's own approach under art 3[16].

7   [*Contd*] (1996) 23 EHRR 413, E Ct HR, paras 145–155. The judgment of the E Ct HR in *Chahal v United Kingdom* led to the creation of the Special Immigration Appeals Commission which now adjudicates in immigration cases which raise national security issues: see the Special Immigration Appeals Commission Act 1997, the Special Immigration Appeals Commission (Procedure) Rules 1998, SI 1998/1881 and *Secretary of State for the Home Department v Rehman* 23 May 2000, unreported, CA.

10   (1999) 29 EHRR 493, E Ct HR.

11   The relief that the Convention requires is 'just satisfaction' (art 41). This does not necessarily include a right to compensation for, or to be relieved of, the consequences of the impugned action. It is not unusual for the E Ct HR to hold that a declaration of a violation is sufficient. See para **2.8.4**.

12   Paragraph 135.

13   The test used by the E Ct HR was that explained by Sir Thomas Bingham MR in the domestic proceedings. He said that the court was not entitled to interfere with the exercise of an administrative discretion on substantive grounds save where the court was satisfied that the decision was unreasonable in the sense that it was beyond the range of responses open to a reasonable decision-maker. In judging whether the decision-maker had exceeded this margin of appreciation, the human rights context was important, so that the more substantial the interference with human rights, the more the court would require by way of justification before it was satisfied that the decision was reasonable: see *R v Ministry of Defence, ex p Smith* [1996] QB 517, at 554, CA. The need for a more intense and anxious judicial scrutiny of administrative decisions which engage fundamental human rights was re-emphasised in *R v Lord Saville, ex p A* [1999] 4 All ER 860, at 870g–872e, CA: see para **1.74** above. The more the threshold of *Wednesbury* irrationality is lowered when fundamental human rights are in play, the easier it will become to establish judicial review as an effective remedy within art 13. On the application of judicial review principles in the light of *Smith and Grady*, see *Turgut v Secretary of State for the Home Department* [2000] Imm AR 306, CA.

14   Paragraph 137.

15   Paragraph 138.

16   Paragraph 138. The same, presumably, could be said of the E Ct HR's judgment in *D v United Kingdom* (1997) 24 EHRR 423 (deportation of a terminal AIDS patient to St Kitts where very limited support and treatment would be available).

4.13.13 [*Contd*] However, in *Keenan v United Kingdom* the EComHR examined the various private law remedies open to the bereaved mother of an individual who had committed suicide as a result of the conditions he had been subjected to in prison. A violation was found because remedies in negligence and under the Fatal Accidents Act 1976 offered no prospect of compensation for the violations of art 3 to which the deceased had been subjected, or for the emotional distress and financial loss that the applicant had suffered as a result of her son's death[3].

1 [*Contd*] *D v United Kingdom* (1997) 24 EHRR 423, E Ct HR, para 71; Application 27798/95 *Amman v Switzerland* (16 February 2000, unreported) para 88, E Ct HR.

2 [*Contd*] But see *Halford v United Kingdom* (1997) 24 EHRR 523, E Ct HR – violation of art 13 where no system of regulating infringements of rights by private bodies, which involved a complaint about the absence of domestic legal regulation of the monitoring by employers of telephone calls made by their employees on office telephones.

3 Application 27229/95 *Keenan v United Kingdom* (6 Sept 1999) paras 90–105, ECommHR; see similarly *TP and KM v United Kingdom* (10 September 1999, unreported) paras 96–102, ECommHR where a failure to provide a remedy for psychiatric distress caused by a violation of art 8, namely unwarranted separation of a mother from her child, amounted to a breach of art 13.

4.13.15 [*Contd*] The police complaints procedure is not sufficiently independent to be an effective remedy: there being no duty on the Chief Constable to refer most complaints into the procedure, officers from the same force carry out the investigation, and members of the Police Complaints Authority are appointed by the Home Secretary and must take account of the guidance he issues[15].

Moreover, the exercise of rights under art 13 must not be unjustifiably hindered by the acts or omissions of the authorities of the state. Where, for example, an individual (or a next-of-kin) has an arguable claim of ill-treatment or unlawful killing by the state in breach of art 3 or art 2, an effective remedy requires not only a thorough and effective investigation but also effective access for the complainant to the investigatory procedure and the payment of compensation where appropriate[16].

15 Application 27237/95 *Govell v United Kingdom* (EComHR, 14 January 1998, para 70, noted at [1999] EHRLR 121) (complaint about unlawful electronic surveillance by the police); *Khan v United Kingdom* (2000) Times, 23 May, E Ct HR.

16 *Assenov v Bulgaria* (1999) 28 EHRR 652, paras 117–118, E Ct HR (ill-treatment by the Bulgarian police, breach of art 13 found); similarly *Velikova v Bulgaria* (18 May 2000), paras 85–90, E Ct HR (breach of art 13 again found). There has also been a number of recent cases against Turkey, particularly by Kurdish applicants: see, for example, *Aydin v Turkey* (1997) 25 EHRR 251, E Ct HR (art 13 includes a requirement for a thorough and effective investigation of credible allegations of rape and ill-treatment in police custody, capable of leading to the identification and punishment of those responsible, and a requirement for effective access to the investigation for the victim), *Mentes v Turkey* (1997) 26 EHRR 595, E Ct HR (arguable claim that homes had been destroyed by agents of the state was not properly investigated) and *Kurt v Turkey* (1999) 27 EHRR 373, E Ct HR (disappearance of applicant's son was not properly investigated by Turkish police and investigating magistrate). In those cases, the investigations appear to have been superficial in the extreme and to have concerned alleged wrong-doing by the state authorities themselves.

4.13.16 The remedy must be available in practice, not just in theory[1]. The remedy must, for example, be available before the implementation of the challenged decision robs it of its effectiveness. Thus, in *Vilvarajah v United Kingdom* the Commission decided that a right of appeal against the refusal of asylum exercisable only from outside the United Kingdom was not effective in practice to consider an allegation that the return itself violated art 3 of the Convention[2]. But in some situations a remedy may be sufficiently effective without being pre-emptive[3].

1   See, generally, *Airey v Ireland* (1979) 2 EHRR 305, E Ct HR. A remedy is not effective within the meaning of art 13 if the public authority to which it is directed refuses to comply: in *Iatridis v Greece* the Greek government had refused to comply with a court ruling upholding the applicant's right to property. Such refusal in practice rendered ineffective an otherwise theoretically good remedy: *Iatrides v Greece* (25 March 1999, unreported), para 66, E Ct HR.

2   (1991) 14 EHRR 248, para 153, EComHR. In practice, the right of appeal would normally have to be exercised from inside the very state where the applicant claimed to fear persecution. The E Ct HR did not consider the point because it was persuaded that judicial review, a remedy capable of having pre-emptive effect, was sufficient. See also *Andersson (M and R) v Sweden* (1992) 14 EHRR 615, E Ct HR, paras 98–103, EComHR.

3   *MS v Sweden* (1998) 28 EHRR 313, paras 54–55, E Ct HR (limited disclosure of medical records to a government agency which was required to maintain confidentiality, subsequent civil and criminal remedies were held to be adequate) and *Barclay v United Kingdom*, EComHR (18 May 1999, unreported) on the adequacy of the remedies for trespass to protect past and prospective invasions of privacy.

7   See para **2.03**, n 6.

4.14
Article 14 Freedom from discrimination in respect of Convention rights

4.14.1 The Convention, unlike other international human rights instruments[1], contains no free-standing guarantee of equal treatment without discrimination[1a]. Instead, art 14 is restricted to a parasitic prohibition of discrimination in relation only to the substantive rights and freedoms set out elsewhere in the Convention. As a result, many important areas of discrimination, notably in the fields of employment[2], and other economic and social rights[3], fall outside the scope of the article.

1a On 26 June 2000, the Committee of Ministers of the Council of Europe agreed the terms of a new Additional Protocol (No 12), creating (by art 1(1)) a new right not to be discriminated against in the 'enjoyment of any right set forth by law' on any ground 'such as sex, race, colour, language, religion, political or other opinion, national or social origin, association with a national minority, property, birth or other status'. The Protocol also prohibits (by art 1(2)) discrimination by public authorities on any of those grounds. The Protocol will be opened for signature on 4 November 2000. It will give additional protection (outside the scope of art 14) where a person is discriminated against (i) in the enjoyment of any right specifically granted to an individual under national law; (ii) in the enjoyment of a right 'which may be inferred from a clear obligation of a public authority under national law' to behave in a particular manner; (iii) by a public authority in the exercise of a discretionary power 'for example, granting certain subsidies'; (iv) by any other act or omission of a public authority 'for example, the behaviour of law enforcement officers when controlling a riot'. (see the Council of Europe's Explanatory Report to Protocol 12, at para 22). The Protocol and Explanatory Report are available at http://www.dhdirhr.coe.fr/.

4.14.2

3 [*Contd*] also *Schröder v Deutsche Telekom AG*, [2000] IRLR 353, 359, para 57 (ECJ describing right to equal pay in art 141 (formerly art 119) of EC Treaty as a 'fundamental human right').

4 Equality of treatment is a principle of lawful administration laid down by the common law: see de Smith, Woolf and Jowell *Judicial Review of Administrative Action* (5th edn, 1995), paras 13-040 to 13-045; *Matadeen v Pointu* [1999] 1 AC 98, per Lord Hoffmann at 26F–G (treating like cases alike and unlike cases differently is a 'general axiom of rational behaviour'); and para **5.15**.

4.14.7

3 For examples, see *Kroon v Netherlands* (1995) 19 EHRR 263, E Ct HR, para 42; *Tinnelly and McElduff v United Kingdom* (1999) 27 EHRR 249, E Ct HR. For another example, see *Larissis v Greece* (1999) 27 EHRR 329, E Ct HR, para 69 (violation of art 9).

4.14.8 Article 14 prohibits discrimination on grounds of sex, race[1], colour, language[1a], religion, political or other opinion, national[2] or social origin, association with a national minority, property, birth or 'other status'. The list of prohibited grounds is, thus, not exhaustive. The term 'other status' includes sexual orientation[3], marital status[4], illegitimacy[5] and professional[6] or military[7] status.

1a See *Williams v Cowell* [2000] 1 WLR 187, CA (language in which court proceedings conducted).

3 [*Contd*] See now *Smith and Grady v United Kingdom* (1999) 29 EHRR 493, E Ct HR and *Lustig-Prean v United Kingdom* (1999) 29 EHRR 548, E Ct HR, (armed forces' policy on discharge of homosexuals violated art 8: Court did not, however, consider separately a complaint of violation of

art 14). It is now quite clear that art 14 prohibits discrimination on grounds of sexual orientation: see also (eg) *Salgueiro da Silva Mouta v Portugal*, judgment of 21 December 1999, E Ct HR. As to domestic law, *Smith v Gardner Merchant* was distinguished in *Pearce v Governing Body of Mayfield School* (2000) Times, 19 April, EAT (gender-specific homophobic abuse did not amount to sex discrimination). See also *Fitzpatrick v Sterling Housing Association Ltd* [1999] 3 WLR 1113, HL (same-sex partner of tenant recognised as part of tenant's family unit for purpose of statutory protection from eviction). Where discrimination on a particular ground (such as sexual orientation or age, as to which, see now the non-statutory Government Code of Practice, Age Diversity in Employment, June 1999) is not unlawful as a matter of domestic law, an employee may nevertheless bring a claim relying upon a contractual equal opportunities policy: see *Taylor v Secretary of State for Scotland* [2000] 3 All ER 90, HL. As to art 13 of the Treaty of Amsterdam, note the European Commission's proposal thereunder dated 31 January 2000 for a Council Directive establishing a general framework for equal treatment in 'employment and occupation' irrespective of 'racial or ethnic origin, religion or belief, disability, age or sexual orientation', and Council Directive 2000/43/EC of 29 June 2000 implementing the principle of equal treatment between persons irrespective of racial or ethnic origin.

4   [*Contd*] See *Re W (Minors) (Abduction: Father's Rights)* [1999] Fam 1, Fam Div (neither English public policy nor the United Kingdom's obligations under art 14 required that the law give unmarried fathers exactly the same rights as married fathers: there was a policy basis for suggesting that some differentiation between them had an objective and reasonable justification).

4.14.9

4   [*Contd*] The question arose again in *R v Lord Chancellor, ex p Lightfoot* [2000] 2 WLR 318, CA, but the court found it unnecessary to rule upon it, having found that no substantive Convention right had been violated.

4.14.12

1   [*Contd*] For a case where the Disability Discrimination Act 1995 effectively required positive discrimination, see *Kent County Council v Mingo* [2000] IRLR 90, EAT (redeployment strategy should have given priority to disabled employee).

4.14.13

1   [*Contd*] For further examples, see *Larissis v Greece* (1999) 27 EHRR 329, E Ct HR, para 68; *Kurt v Turkey* (1999) 27 EHRR 373, E Ct HR, para 147; *Kaya v Turkey* (1999) 28 EHRR 1, E Ct HR, para 113.

4.14.16

1   [*Contd*] See also *Canea Catholic Church v Greece* (1999) 27 EHRR 521, E Ct HR, para 47 (violation found as no justification put forward).

4.16

Article 16 Restrictions on the political rights of aliens

4.16.1 [*Contd*] *Piermont v France*[3] remains the only case yet to have reached the E Ct HR under art 16. But, in an allied context, there has been a recent sign that the very limited impact of art 16 will be reduced still further by the introduction of European citizenship under the Maastricht Treaty (EC Treaty art 8(1))[4]. Moreover, where the alien in question is a European citizen, it is likely that art 16 will have to yield to the powerful prohibition of discrimination on grounds of nationality imposed by European Community law[5]. In short, art 16 is looking increasingly anachronistic.

3   (1995) 20 EHRR 301, E Ct HR.
4   *Matthews v United Kingdom* (1999) 28 EHRR 361, E Ct HR (where the prohibition of a British citizen, resident in Gibraltar, from voting in the 1994 European Parliament elections was held to violate art 3 of the First Protocol) discussed at para **4.21.7**.
5   EC Treaty, art 12.

4.19

Article 1 of the First Protocol Right to property

4.19.2 [*Contd*] In *Iatridis v Greece*[10] the clientele of a cinema were held to constitute an asset falling within the protection of art 1 of the Protocol[11].

10 (25 March 1999, unreported) E Ct HR.
11 Paragraph 54.

4.19.6 [*Contd*] For the principle that art 1 of the Protocol comprises three distinct rules, see also *Beyeler v Italy*[3].

3 (5 January 2000, unreported) para 98, E Ct HR.

4.19.9 [*Contd*] *Vasilescu v Romania* is now reported[2]. See also *Brumarescu v Romania*[3], where the E Ct HR reiterated that in determining whether there has been a deprivation of possessions within the second rule, it is necessary to look behind the appearances and investigate the realities of the situation complained of, in order to ascertain whether there has been a de facto expropriation[4]. See further *Grape Bay Ltd v A-G of Bermuda*[5], where Lord Hoffmann, for the Privy Council, observed that: 'whether a law or exercise of an administrative power does amount to a deprivation of property depends of course on the substance of the matter rather than upon the form in which the law is drafted.'[6]

2 (1999) 28 EHRR 241.
3 (28 October 1999, unreported) E Ct HR.
4 Paragraph 76.
5 [2000] 1 WLR 574.
6 At 583G.

4.19.17 [*Contd*] The availability of compensation may also be relevant in assessing whether the requisite fair balance has been struck in relation to an interference falling within the first or third rule of art 1 of the Protocol[2].

2 See *Chassagnou v France* (2000) 29 EHRR 615, E Ct HR, para 82; *Immobiliare Saffi v Italy* (28 July 1999, unreported) E Ct HR, para 57; and *AO v Italy* (30 May 2000, unreported), para 28, E Ct HR.

4.19.19 [*Contd*] In *Iatridis v Greece*[2] the E Ct HR emphasised that the first and most important requirement of art 1 of the First Protocol is that any interference by a public authority with the peaceful enjoyment of possessions should be lawful[3]

2 (25 March 1999, unreported).
3 Paragraph 58. See also *Beyeler v Italy* (5 January 2000, unreported) para 108, E Ct HR; and *Belvedere Alberghiera srl v Italy* (30 May 2000, unreported), para 56, E Ct HR.

4.19.20 [*Contd*] When speaking of 'law', art 1 of the First Protocol alludes to the same concept to be found elsewhere in the Convention, a concept which comprises statutory law as well as case law. It implies qualitative requirements, notably those of accessibility and foreseeability[2].

2 See *Spacek v Czech Republic* (9 November 1999, unreported), para 54, E Ct HR.

4.20

Article 2 of the First Protocol
Right to Education

4.20.1 [*Contd*] The right to education does not guarantee a particular standard of education[5].

5   *R v Secretary of State for the Home Department, ex p Holub* (8 October 1999, unreported) (Mr Justice Carnwath).

4.20.5

13   [*Contd*] See also Application 14524/89 *Yanasik v Turkey* 74 DR 14 (1993) EComHR.

4.20.6 [*Contd*] See *R v Secretary of State for the Home Department, ex p Holub*[14].

1   [*Contd*] See also *Ford v United Kingdom* [1996] EHRLR 534, EComHR.
14   Paragraph **4.20.1** above.

4.20.8 Although the right to education does not guarantee a particular standard of education, it does imply a right to the reasonable enjoyment of existing institutions within any country without unjustified discrimination[7].

7   *R v Secretary of State for the Home Department, ex p Holub*, para **4.20.1** above.

4.20.11

1   See *Eriksson v Sweden* (1989) 12 EHRR 183, E Ct HR, para 93.

4.20.15

1   [*Contd*] See also *Ford v United Kingdom*, para **4.20.6** above.

4.21

Article 3 of the First Protocol
Right to free elections

4.21.7 In *Matthews v United Kingdom*[1], the E Ct HR held that the denial of the right to vote in the election of members of the European Parliament in Gibraltar in 1994 violated art 3 of the First Protocol. The United Kingdom had a duty to 'secure' elections to the European Parliament notwithstanding the Community character of the election. Although acts of the EC as such could not be challenged before the E Ct HR because the EC is not a Contracting Party, the Convention does not exclude the transfer of competences to international organisations provided that Convention rights continue to be secured. Member States' responsibility therefore continues even after such a transfer. The E Ct HR recalled that the word 'legislature' in art 3 does not necessarily mean the national parliament; the word has to be interpreted in the light of the constitutional structure of the State in question. To interpret the sphere of activities of the European Parliament as falling outside the scope of art 3 would risk undermining one of the fundamental tools by which effective political democracy can be maintained. Since the coming into force of the TEU (the Maastricht Treaty), the European Parliament has moved away from being a purely consultative body towards being a body with a decisive role to play in the legislative process of the EC. It represents the principal form of democratic, political accountability in the Community system, and is sufficiently involved in the specific legislative processes leading to the passage of legislation under art 189b and art 189c of the EC Treaty, and is sufficiently involved in the general democratic supervision of the activities of the EC, to constitute part of the 'legislature' of Gibraltar for the purposes of art 3. The rights set out in art 3 may be the subject of limitations. The Contracting States enjoy a wide margin of appreciation in imposing conditions on the right to vote, but such conditions must not curtail the right to vote to such an extent as to impair its very essence and deprive it of effectiveness. The applicant had been completely denied any opportunity to express her opinion in the choice of the members of the European Parliament and there had been a violation of her rights under art 3. The position was not analogous to that of persons who are unable to take part in elections because they live outside the jurisdiction, as such individuals have weakened the link between themselves and the jurisdiction.

1   (1999) 28 EHRR 361, E Ct HR.

4.21.8 In response to the decision in *Matthews*, the Government within a month tabled an amendment to the 1976 EC Act on direct elections in order to extend the European franchise to Gibraltar[1]. Negotiations on this amendment are ongoing.

1   598 HL Official Report (5th series) (11 March 1999), WA 45.

Chapter 5
Scotland

5.05 [*Contd*] The sifting procedure whereby the court decides whether to grant leave to appeal was considered under art 6 in *Martin v United Kingdom*[9].

9   1999 SCCR 941.

5.09

1   [*Contd*] An application for revision of the *McGinley and Egan* judgment was refused by the E Ct HR in *McGinley and Egan v UK (No 2)* (11 January 2000, unreported).

5.20 [*Contd*] Other criminal cases have concerned the adequacy of legal aid[7], and the procedural rules governing the raising of a devolution issue[8].

6   [*Contd*] *Al Megrahi v Times Newspapers Ltd* 1999 SCCR 824.
7   *Gayne v Vannet* 2000 SCCR 5.
8   *HM Advocate v Dickson* 1999 SCCR 859.

5.21 [*Contd*] The Convention has also been considered in numerous cases concerned with immigration[3]. The dismissal of an action on the ground of irrelevancy has also been considered in the light of art 6[4].

3   eg *Abdadou v Secretary of State for the Home Department*, 1998 SC 504; *Akhtar v Secretary of State for the Home Department* (23 March 2000, unreported) (Court of Session).
4   *Crooks v Haddow* (1 March 2000, unreported) (Court of Session).

5.23 [*Contd*] It should be borne in mind that the Convention is not the only human rights instrument which is relevant to the Scottish Parliament and Executive: see eg SA 1998 Sch 5, Pt I, para 7(2).

5.28

1   [*Contd*] see *Whaley v Lord Watson of Invergowrie* 2000 SLT 475.
2   [*Contd*] see *Whaley v Lord Watson of Invergowrie* 2000 SLT 475.

5.31 [*Contd*] For example, since the Sheriff Courts (Scotland) Act 1971 conferred on the Secretary of State a power to appoint temporary sheriffs which was incompatible with the Convention, that power was not transferred to the Scottish Ministers but remained with the Secretary of State[1].

1   *Starrs v Ruxton* 1999 SCCR 1052, 1079–1080, 1100; 1999 SCCR 941–1101.

5.32 [*Contd*] Compliance with the Convention is thus made by the SA 1998 into a question of vires. Undue delay in bringing a person to trial, for example, is not something which can be reflected in the sentence imposed, as the European Court of Justice has decided in a case concerned with art 6[2], or for which compensation might be awarded: it operates as a bar to further prosecution[3].

Nevertheless, the right to object under the SA 1998 to a violation of the Convention can be waived[4].

1 [*Contd*] It has been held not to be restricted to the initiation of a criminal prosecution: *HM Advocate v Robb* 1999 SCCR 971, 975. On the interpretation of HRA 1998, s 6, see *HM Advocate v Robb* 1999 SCCR 971, 975; *Starrs v Ruxton* 1999 SCCR 1052, 1080, 1104-1105.
2 Case C–185/95 *Baustahlgewebe v Commission* (17 December 1998, unreported), ECJ.
3 See cases cited in para **5.43G**.
4 *Clancy v Caird*, 2000 SLT 546.

5.32A The term 'act' in s 57(2) has generally been given a wide construction. In the context of criminal proceedings, it has been held to include the Lord Advocate's moving the court to grant a remedy[1]; and, generally, all actions taken or avoided by the Lord Advocate in the course of the prosecution of offences[2]. It has been held (both in civil and criminal proceedings) to include a failure to act[3]. It has been treated (by concession) as including the initiation[4] and continuation[5] of a prosecution; the calling of an indictment[6]; the leading of evidence[7]; and an application for a confiscation order[8]; but it has been held not to include the Lord Advocate's informal involvement in administrative arrangements for the transmission of trial proceedings by closed circuit television, the transmission having been authorised by the court and the arrangements being under the supervision of the court[9]. This approach is consistent with the intention[10] that the Scottish Executive should have no power to take executive action which is incompatible with the Convention. It has the effect however of preventing a prosecution from being conducted on the basis of domestic law (including Acts of Parliament) – the law of evidence, for example, or the statutory basis of appointment of the judiciary– whenever the domestic law fails to meet Convention requirements[11]. The case of *Starrs v Ruxton*[12] illustrates the point: the court could not strike down the UK legislation under which temporary sheriffs were appointed, or even make a declaration of its incompatibility with the Convention; but it being conceded that the prosecution of accused persons before a temporary sheriff was an 'act' of the Lord Advocate, that act could be held to be incompatible with the Convention and therefore incompetent.

1 *HM Advocate v Scottish Media Newspapers Ltd* 1999 SCCR 599, 603.
2 *HM Advocate v Robb* 1999 SCCR 971, 976.
3 *HM Advocate v Robb* 1999 SCCR, 975; *Clancy v Caird* 2000 SLT 546.
4 *HM Advocate v Robb* 1999 SCCR 971.
5 *Starrs v Ruxton* 1999 SCCR 1052; *McNab v HM Advocate* 1999 SCCR 930; *McLean v HM Advocate* 2000 SCCR 112; *Paton v Ritchie* 2000 SCCR 151; *Buchanan v McLean* (15 June 2000, unreported) (High Court of Justiciary).
6 *HM Advocate v Little* 1999 SCCR 625.
7 *HM Advocate v Robb* 1999 SCCR 971, 976; *Paton v Ritchie* 2000 SCCR 151, 154; *McKenna v HM Advocate* 2000 SCCR 159. A devolution issue can competently challenge the giving of notice of an intention to lead evidence, although it will normally (but not invariably) be premature to raise the issue prior to trial: see the cases cited (which might be contrasted with *HM Advocate v Campbell* 1999 SCCR 980, 983). This is discussed further at para **5.43D** below.
8 *McSalley v HM Advocate* (10 April 2000, unreported) (High Court of Justiciary).
9 *British Broadcasting Corporation, Petitioners (No 2)* 2000 SCCR 533. See also *Hoekstra v HM Advocate* (2 June 2000, unreported) (High Court of Justiciary).
10 See para **5.23**.
11 Subject to the limited exception provided by SA 1998, s 57(3): as to which, see *Starrs v Ruxton* 1999 SCCR 1052.
12 1999 SCCR 1052.

5.33 [*Contd*] The acts of members of the Procurator Fiscal service have in practice been treated as the acts of the Lord Advocate[2].

2   *Starrs v Ruxton* 1999 SCCR 1052, 1061, 1084; *Buchanan v McLean* (15 June 2000, unreported) (High Court of Justiciary).

5.42 [*Contd*] Rules have been issued, and are discussed below.

5.43A   Subordinate legislation has been made regulating the procedure to be followed where a devolution issue is sought to be raised. The present discussion will focus on the rules applicable to criminal proceedings in Scotland[1], and to civil proceedings before the Court of Session[2]. There are also rules in respect of civil proceedings in the Sheriff Court[3] and in respect of proceedings before the Judicial Committee[4].

1   Act of Adjournal (Devolution Issue Rules) 1999, SI 1999/1346, as amended by Act of Adjournal (Criminal Procedure Rules Amendment) (Miscellaneous) 2000, SI 2000/65. The 1999 Act of Adjournal inserted a new Chapter 40 in the Act of Adjournal (Criminal Procedure Rules) 1996, SI 1996/513.
2   Act of Sederunt (Devolution Issue Rules) 1999, SI 1999/1345, as amended by Act of Sederunt (Rules of the Court of Session Amendment) (Miscellaneous) 2000, SI 2000/66. The 1999 Act of Sederunt inserted a new Chapter 25A in the Act of Sederunt (Rules of the Court of Session) 1994, SI 1994/1443.
3   Act of Sederunt (Proceedings for Determination of Devolution Issues Rules) 1999, SI 1999/1347.
4   The Judicial Committee (Devolution Issues) Rules Order 1999, SI 1999/665.

5.43B   So far as criminal proceedings are concerned, the rules are contained in Chapter 40 of the 1996 Act of Adjournal (as amended). In relation to proceedings on indictment, the Act of Adjournal requires a party to those proceedings who proposes to raise a devolution issue to give notice within 7 days of service of the indictment. The notice must give sufficient specification of the devolution issue to enable the court to determine whether any devolution issue actually arises[1]. The notice has to be given to the court, the other parties to the proceedings and the Advocate General[2]. The devolution issue is then to be considered at a hearing held in accordance with the procedure followed under existing law[3]. A challenge to a provision in an act of the Scottish Parliament as being incompatible with any of the Convention rights might, for example, take the form of a plea to the competency or relevancy of an indictment based on the provision. A complaint that the Lord Advocate was acting in a manner which was incompatible with Convention rights might take the form of a plea of oppression. In either case, the issue could (and normally should) be dealt with, in solemn proceedings in the High Court, at a preliminary diet[4]. For such a diet to be held, notice normally has to be given within 15 days of service of the indictment: the shorter period allowed in respect of a devolution issue may reflect the need to notify the Advocate General (who is likely to have no prior knowledge of the proceedings) in adequate time for the hearing[5]. These relatively short time limits generally reflect the tight timetable of solemn procedure, which requires the indictment to be served 29 days prior to the trial[6], and envisages the holding of any preliminary diet during the intervening period. A broadly similar procedure applies where a party wishes to raise a devolution issue in summary proceedings[7] or in other types of criminal proceedings[8]. A devolution issue cannot be raised in criminal proceedings except in accordance with these time limits, unless the court on cause shown otherwise determines[9]. Following the service of the notice, the court may determine that no devolution issue in fact arises[10]. If a devolution issue does arise, then the court can determine it, or it can make a reference to the High Court of Justiciary (unless the court itself consists of two or more judges of the High Court of Justiciary[11], in which case a reference can be made to the Judicial Committee of the Privy Council)[12]. The one exception is that where a court determines that a devolution issue may be raised during a trial, it cannot make a reference, but must determine the issue itself. This avoids what might otherwise be insuperable practical problems[13]. The scheme of the Act of Adjournal is directed towards ensuring that devolution issues are raised prior to trial, whenever possible. This partly reflects the practical problems which would arise, as just mentioned, if devolution issues were to be raised during a trial. It may also reflect the fact that an erroneous determination of a devolution issue during a trial leading to an acquittal in proceedings on indictment could not be appealed so as to affect the acquittal[14]. The Act of Adjournal has been challenged as being ultra vires, on the basis inter alia that the time limits are incompatible with the Convention. The challenge was unsuccessful[15].

1   Rule 40.6.
2   Rule 40.2(1).
3   This is implied rather than expressed: see *HM Advocate v Montgomery* 1999 SCCR 959.
4   Under the Criminal Procedure (Scotland) Act 1995, s 72. See *HM Advocate v Montgomery* 1999 SCCR 959; *Buchanan v McLean* (15 June 2000, unreported) (High Court of Justiciary). In solemn proceedings in the Sheriff Court, the issue could be dealt with at a first diet: 1995 Act, s 71(2).
5   The Advocate General has 7 days from receipt of a notice to decide whether to become a party to the proceedings: Rule 40.2(3).
6   1995 Act, s 66(6).
7   Rule 40.3.
8   Rule 40.4. This would cover petitions to the nobile officium. It may also cover appeals.
9   Rule 40.5. As to what constitutes 'cause shown', see *HM Advocate v Montgomery* 1999 SCCR 959. As that case indicates (at 965D), 'ordinary' time limits or rules may apply as well as the particular requirements imposed by Ch 40 of the Act of Adjournal.
10 Rules 40.2(2), 40.3(2) and 40.4(3).
11 Rule 40.7(1).
12 Rule 40.9(1).
13 If, for example, a devolution issue were raised during a trial before a jury, and a reference were made, the jury would have to be sent away while the case was dealt with before the High Court of Justiciary (and, possibly, the Judicial Committee). The adjournment of the trial would be liable to last weeks, if not months, making it impractical to resume the trial (even assuming the jury could be re-assembled).
14 The Lord Advocate cannot appeal against an acquittal in proceedings on indictment: 1995 Act, s 106(1). He can however refer a point of law which has arisen in relation to a charge to the High Court for its opinion; but the opinion does not affect the acquittal: s 123. He also has a limited right of appeal against procedural decisions during the course of proceedings on indictment: s 131. The Advocate General has a right to refer any devolution issue to the High Court for its opinion, following an acquittal or a conviction; but the opinion does not affect the acquittal or conviction: s 288A (inserted by the SA 1998, Sch 8, para 32). A decision taken prior to trial can be appealed: 1995 Act, s 74.
15 *HM Advocate v Dickson* 1999 SCCR 859.

5.43C   The new rules applicable to civil proceedings in the Court of Session[1] adopt a broadly similar scheme. The devolution issue must be specified in detail in pleadings. The issue must be raised before any evidence is led, unless the court on cause shown otherwise determines[2]. Intimation of the devolution issue must be given to the Lord Advocate and to the Advocate General[3], who then have 14 days to decide whether to take part in the proceedings[4], and a further 7 days to lodge written submissions[5]. The issue is then dealt with at a hearing before proof or trial. This procedure is in some respects analogous to the procedure followed in the Court of Session under existing practice where a party wishes to raise a preliminary point (eg as to jurisdiction or title to sue) or a question of relevancy.

1 Act of Sederunt (Devolution Issues Rules) 1999, SI 1999/1345. As to the Sheriff Court, see the Act of Sederunt (Proceedings for Determination of Devolution Issues Rules) 1999, SI 1999/1347.
2 Rule 25A.3(1).
3 Rule 25A.5(1).
4 Rule 25A.5(4).
5 Rule 25A.6(1).

5.43D In both criminal and civil procedure, then, the rules aim to ensure, as far as possible, that devolution issues are raised and determined prior to trial. In practice, however, this may not always be possible: there may be situations where the devolution issue cannot reasonably be identified in advance of trial; and even if the devolution issue can be identified prior to trial, it may not always be possible to determine it until the significance of the point raised can be assessed in the context of the trial. This is liable in particular to be a difficulty in relation to issues relating to evidence. In general, the court's role in ruling on the admissibility of evidence and directing the jury (if any) on the use to be made of evidence should operate, at the trial, as a means of preventing evidence being tendered and relied upon in such a way as to deprive an accused person of a fair trial[1]. For that reason, questions under art 6 relating to the admissibility of evidence should generally be raised at the trial[2]. There are however circumstances in which a devolution issue relating to evidence can be raised and determined prior to trial[3].

1 *HM Advocate v Robb* 1999 SCCR 971, 977; *HM Advocate v Campbell* 1999 SCCR 980; *Paton v Ritchie* 1999 SCCR 151.
2 Ibid.
3 See eg *Brown v Stott* 2000 SCCR 314.

5.43E There appears to have been, as at the date of writing, only one case in which legislation passed by the Scottish Parliament has been challenged as being incompatible with the Convention[1]. The challenge, which concerned the Mental Health (Public Safety & Appeals) (Scotland) Act 1999[2], was unsuccessful.

1 *A v Scottish Ministers* 2000 SLT 873. The challenge was based on art 5(1)(e) and (4) of the Convention.
2 1999 asp 1.

5.43F There appears to have been, as at the date of writing, only one other civil case before the Court of Session in which a devolution issue has been raised. In that case, the independence of a temporary judge was challenged, unsuccessfully[1]. In another case, before an Employment Tribunal, the exclusion of Employment Tribunals from the legal aid scheme was held not to raise a devolution issue[2].

1 *Clancy v Caird*, 2000 SLT 546.
2 *Gerrie v Ministry of Defence* (22 October 1999, unreported) (Employment Tribunal at Glasgow).

5.43G The criminal courts, on the other hand, have had to deal with a great many cases in which devolution issues have been raised, some of which have been of considerable importance. The principal issues raised relating to the Convention can be summarised as follows:

(1) Whether a criminal trial can take place before a temporary sheriff, the point being whether the temporary sheriff possesses sufficient independence to comply with art 6[1].

(2) Whether a summary criminal trial can take place compatibly with art 6(1) when the legal aid available to the defence is based on fixed fees which are said to be inadequate[2].

(3) Whether there has been excessive delay in the proceedings, contrary to art 6(1)[3].

(4) Whether the Crown can use as evidence against an accused a statement which he was required to provide to the police under s 172 of the Road Traffic Act 1988[4].

(5) Whether the Crown can, consistently with art 6(1), lead evidence of a police interview with the accused[5], or of an identification parade[6], the accused not having had access to a solicitor during the interview or identification parade.

(6) Whether pre-trial publicity has prevented the holding of a trial which would be compatible with art 6[7].

(7) Whether hearsay evidence can be admitted[8].

(8) Whether the statutory presumptions applicable where a confiscation order is sought in respect of the proceeds of drug trafficking are incompatible with art 6(2) of the Convention or with art 1 of the First Protocol[9].

There have also been cases concerning the granting of a search warrant[10]; the impartiality of a judge[11] or a jury[12]; the refusal of bail[13]; contempt of court[14]; the specification of criminal charges[15]; a visit by a jury to the locus of an offence[16]; the disclosure of a prior conviction during the course of a trial[17]; the consequences of a procedural irregularity during the course of appeal proceedings[18]; and the broadcasting of trial proceedings[19].

1 *Starrs v Ruxton* 1999 SCCR 1052.
2 *Buchanan v McLean (15 June 2000, unreported) (High Court of Justiciary).*
3 *HM Advocate v Little* 1999 SCCR 625; *McNab v HM Advocate* 1999 SCCR 930; *McLean v HM Advocate* 2000 SCCR 112; *Docherty v HM Advocate* (14 January 2000, unreported) (High Court of Justiciary); *Robb v HM Advocate* 2000 SCCR 354; *HM Advocate v McGlinchey & Rennicks* (18 February 2000, unreported) (High Court of Justiciary); *Crummock (Scotland) Ltd v HM Advocate* 2000 SCCR 453; *HM Advocate v Hynd* (9 May 2000, unreported) (High Court of Justiciary).
4 *Brown v Stott* 2000 SCCR 314.
5 *HM Advocate v Robb* 1999 SCCR 971; *Paton v Ritchie* 2000 SCCR 151.
6 *HM Advocate v Campbell* 1999 SCCR 980.
7 *Montgomery v HM Advocate (No 2)* (16 November 1999, unreported) (High Court of Justiciary); *HM Advocate v Fraser* 2000 SCCR 412.
8 *McKenna v HM Advocate* 2000 SCCR 159; *HM Advocate v Nulty* 2000 SCCR 431.
9 *McSalley v HM Advocate* (10 April 2000, unreported) (High Court of Justiciary).
10 *Birse v HM Advocate* 2000 SCCR 505.
11 *Hoekstra v HM Advocate (No 2)* 2000 SCCR 367.
12 *Crummock (Scotland) Ltd v HM Advocate* 2000 SCCR 453.
13 *Burt, Petitioner* 2000 SCCR 384; also *Brown v Selfridge* 2000 SLT 437.
14 *HM Advocate v Scottish Media Newspapers Ltd* 1999 SCCR 599.
15 *McLean v HM Advocate* 2000 SCCR 112.
16 *Hoekstra v HM Advocate* 2000 SCCR 263.
17 *Andrew v HM Advocate* 2000 SLT 402.
18 *Hoekstra v HM Advocate* 2000 SCCR 263.
19 *British Broadcasting Corpn, Petitioners (No 2)* 2000 SCCR 533.

5.46B An important transitional provision, to cover the period between the coming into force of the SA 1998 and the date when the HRA 1998 is fully enforced, is s 129(2). It provides that during that transitional period, ss 29(2)(d), 57(2) and (3), 100 and 126(1) and Sch 6 to the SA 1998 are to have effect as they will have effect after the time when the HRA 1998 is fully in force.

Chapter 6
Northern Ireland

6.07 [*Contd*] With the European Commission of Human Rights having been finally abolished as from 1 November 1999, it no longer makes sense to distinguish between applications to Strasbourg which reach only the European Commission and those which go all the way to the European Court of Human Rights. In addition to the eight European Court cases concerning Northern Irish law identified in this and the following six paragraphs in the main text, there are now eight further European Court cases to note.

6.07A In *Kerr v United Kingdom*[1] the issue was whether a man arrested under the Prevention of Terrorism (Temporary Provisions) Act 1989, on suspicion of being involved in the commission, preparation or instigation of acts of terrorism, had been provided in time with further details of the evidence against him. Seven days after his arrest, he was charged with possession of 'any record or document likely to be useful to terrorists'. The police alleged that it would have been clear to Mr Kerr, from the 39 interviews he had been subjected to during his week's detention, what kinds of record or document (namely computer disks carrying information about electoral lists and police and army matters) were in question. The European Court held that the application was inadmissible in so far as it alleged a breach of art 5(2) of the Convention (the right to be informed promptly of the reasons for one's arrest and of the charges one might face) but that the application should be communicated to the United Kingdom government for consideration of the position under art 5(3) (the right of a detainee to be brought promptly before a judicial officer) and under art 5(5) (the right to compensation if any art 5 right is breached).

1   Application 40451/98.

6.08 [*Contd*] In *Jordan v United Kingdom, Kelly v United Kingdom, McKerr v United Kingdom* and *Shanaghan v United Kingdom*[2] the applications mainly concern art 2 of the Convention: a number of families are alleging that the security forces in Northern Ireland failed adequately to protect the right to life of their loved ones. Central to the applications is the suggestion that the state does not have in place an adequate system for investigating deaths. The inquest system, for example, is alleged to be fundamentally flawed because the Crown can prevent information being presented by claiming public interest immunity. In making their arguments, the applicants are relying on recent statements by the European Court in cases involving Turkey, especially *Kaya v Turkey*[3]. The Northern Ireland Human Rights Commission, whose functions are outlined in paras **6.38** to **6.44**, applied for and was granted permission to make a submission as an interested third party. The submission[4] relies heavily upon the jurisprudence of the Inter-American Court of Human Rights and argues that the inquest system, the prosecution system and the civil compensation system are all not sufficient in Northern Ireland to satisfy the requirements of art 2. On 4 April 2000, after an oral hearing relating to the group of cases, the European Court held all of the applications to be admissible.

2   Application 24746/94, 30054/96, 28883/95 and 37715/97.
3   (1999) 28 EHRR 1.
4   Available on the Commission's website at www.nihrc.org.

6.08A   In *Caraher v United Kingdom*[1], the applicant's husband was killed by British soldiers while he was in a car driven by his brother. The soldiers were tried for murder but were acquitted by the judge on the basis that there was a reasonable possibility that the soldiers had fired at the driver because they honestly considered this to be necessary in order to save a fellow soldier from being run over by the car. The applicant then started civil proceedings to obtain compensation and a settlement was reached under which she was paid £50,000 by the Ministry of Defence. The applicant claimed this was not an adequate remedy but the European Court rejected her claim, remarking that it was the applicant's own choice to accept that sum and that the risk of having to pay costs if she had proceeded with her action was a normal feature of civil proceedings. The Court also rejected the argument that the United Kingdom was operating an administrative practice, contrary to art 2 of the Convention, whereby it offered compensation to the families of victims shot by the security forces (supposedly to buy them off). The Court could find no convincing evidence of such a practice. The applicant could not therefore claim to be a victim and her application was rejected as being manifestly ill-founded.

1   Application 24520/94; decision of 11 January 2000.

6.08B   On 6 June 2000 the European Court decided two further important cases concerning the right to defend oneself through legal assistance and the right to silence. In *Magee v United Kindgom*[1] the applicant had been denied access to a solicitor for more than 48 hours after his arrest. During that period he was questioned intensely by rotating teams of detectives about his part in an attempted bomb attack on military personnel. He was cautioned at each interview that he was not obliged to answer questions but that his failure to mention any fact which he later relied on in his defence in court might be treated in court as supporting any other relevant evidence against him. After about 32 hours of questioning he signed a lengthy confession statement. He was later convicted at a trial before a judge sitting alone and an appeal to the Court of Appeal was unsuccessful. In *Averill v United Kingdom*[2] the applicant had been denied access to a solicitor during the first 24 hours of his detention. He too was questioned and cautioned during that period, but he did not say anything. At his trial, however, the judge (again sitting without a jury) drew a very strong inference from the applicant's silence during that initial questioning and convicted him. The Court of Appeal of Northern Ireland again rejected an appeal[3]. In both cases, the European Court held that the applicants' rights under art 6(3)(c) – the right to defend oneself in person or through legal assistance – had been breached. They reaffirmed what the Court had said about access to legal assistance in *Murray v United Kingdom*[4], even though the denial of access to a solicitor in the *Averill* case was for a shorter period than in *Murray*. In *Magee*, a relevant factor was the nature of the conditions in the Castlereagh holding centre where the applicant was detained (Mr Averill was detained in the slightly better conditions of Gough Barracks holding centre). Drawing upon findings made by the European Committee for the Prevention of

Torture and Inhuman or Degrading Treatment and Punishment, the Court in *Magee* said, at para 43, that:

> 'the austerity of the conditions of his detention and his exclusion from outside contact were intended to be psychologically coercive and conducive to breaking down any resolve he may have manifested at the beginning of his detention to remain silent...[T]he applicant, as a matter of procedural fairness, should have been given access to a solicitor at the initial stages of the interrogation as a counterweight to the intimidating atmosphere specifically devised to sap his will and make him confide in his interrogators.'

In both cases, moreover, the Court felt that the very caution administered to the applicants added to the oppression they were suffering because it put them in a dilemma as to whether or not to answer any questions before getting access to a solicitor. It is now difficult to see how denying access to solicitors to persons arrested under the anti-terrorist legislation in Northern Ireland can continue without in almost every case a breach of art 6(3)(c) occurring.

1   Available on the European Court's website.
2   Available on the European Court's website.
3   Mr Averill escaped from prison in December 1997 and is still unlawfully at large.
4   (1996) 22 EHRR 29. See para **6.11**.

6.08C   The European Court went on to hold, however, in both *Magee v United Kingdom* and *Averill v United Kingdom*, that no other breaches of the Convention had occurred (and nor was any compensation for non-pecuniary loss awarded). In *Magee*, there was no breach of art 14 just because persons arrested under the same anti-terrorist legislation in England and Wales are entitled to immediate access to a solicitor: differences in the law based on geographical location rather than on personal characteristics cannot be violative of the Convention. In *Averill*, the Court held, with one dissenting voice[1], that there had been no breach of art 6(2) of the Convention as regards the drawing of inferences from the applicant's silence in the face of questioning. The Court reiterated its approach stated in *Murray*[2] and concluded that on the facts of the case infront of it, there as nothing unfair in the drawing of inferences. The prosecution case against the applicant was otherwise already strong, especially the incriminating forensic evidence, and the applicant's and his witness' testimony to the court had in effect only served to weaken the case for the defence.

1   That of Judge Loucaides, from Cyprus (who also dissented in *Murray v UK*). For him, the right to silence is an absolute right.
2   (1996) 22 EHRR 29. See para **6.11**.

6.10   [*Contd*] The Terrorism Act 2000, which will be brought into force early in 2001, retains the seven-day detention power provided for in the former Prevention of Terrorism (Temporary Provisions) Acts, but subjects it to judicial oversight after (at the latest) four days. This ought to allow the UK Government to withdraw its notices of derogation from art 5(3) of the European Convention and art 9(3) of the UN's International Covenant on Civil and Political Rights. Pending the withdrawal of these notices of derogation the UK Government is still vulnerable if someone is arrested and detained for more than four days because it is increasingly difficult for the Government to argue convincingly that there is a public emergency threatening the life of the nation in Northern Ireland[5]. In the context of a court challenge to the early release scheme for prisoners, set up by statute[6] as a result of the Belfast (Good Friday) Agreement in 1998[7], the

Government itself has successfully defended its view that the paramilitary ceasefires are holding in Northern Ireland: neither the High Court nor the Court of Appeal could find any irrationality in that conclusion[8].

5 In the last quarter of 1999, eight persons were detained for more than four days in Northern Ireland: Research and Statistical Bulletin 1/2000, Tale 5 (Northern Ireland Office).
6 Northern Ireland (Sentences) Act 1998.
7 Cmnd 3883.
8 *Re Williamson's Application* [2000] NI 281.

6.11 [*Contd*] The guidelines mentioned at the end of this paragraph have now been translated into legal provisions by virtue of the Criminal Evidence (NI) Order 1999, art 36.

6.15 [*Contd*] Although the European Convention has, in effect, been in force in Northern Ireland as far as actions by the Northern Ireland Assembly, Executive and Departments are concerned since the inception of devolution (2 December 1999)[6], it seems that no court proceedings in respect of those actions have yet been commenced. However, in one case the High Court did quash a vesting order made by a Government department partly because the Department had not met the standards of consultation required by art 6 of the Convention[7]. In an earlier case the Court of Appeal of Northern Ireland refused to hold that delaying access to a solicitor in a way which breached art 6 of the Convention meant that the detainee had a right to damages for breach of statutory duty[8]. *In re Ferris' Application*[9], Gillen J granted leave to apply for judicial review to an applicant who was relying upon his rights as a parent, under art 2 of the First Protocol to the European Convention, to ensure that his daughter was educated in accordance with his religious and philosophical convictions (he objected to an integrated school teaching his daughter Gaelic studies). In a case recently decided in the High Court in May 2000, Kerr J refused to find any breach of the Convention in a requirement that prospective Queen's Counsel must sign a declaration which, as in England and Wales, included the phrase 'I will well and truly serve Her Majesty Queen Elizabeth II and all whom I may be lawfully called upon to serve'; he held that it did not violate arts 9, 10 or 14, primarily because it did not discriminate against anyone even on the basis of their political opinion[10]. (Kerr J did find that the decision by the Lord Chancellor to retain the requirement to take the declaration was unreasonable in the *Wednesbury* sense, as it was based on a misunderstanding of the facts and a failure to recognise that it would prove controversial). In June 2000, the Lord Chancellor announced that he was altering the required declaration so that it would no longer make any specific reference to the Queen. As a result of *Starrs v Ruxton* case in Scotland[11], the Lord Chancellor announced changes to the terms of service of part-time judicial office-holders in Northern Ireland, including deputy resident magistrates, deputy county court judges and deputy district judges[12]. He later announced new conditions of service for part-time Tribunal appointments and said that the First and deputy First Ministers in Northern Ireland were being invited to agree that these arrangements be brought before the Executive Committee with a view to an announcement being made to the Assembly by the relevant Northern Ireland Ministers[13].

6 During the period of the Northern Ireland Assembly's suspension (11 February to 30 May 2000), the Northern Ireland Departments were still obliged to comply with the European Convention: see Northern Ireland Act 2000, s 1.
7 *Cowan v Department of Economic Development* [2000] NI 122.

8   *Cullen v Chief Constable of the RUC* [1999] 10 Bulletin of Northern Ireland Law s 21 (16 June 1999).
9   (22 June 2000, unreported).
10 *Re Treacy's and Macdonald's Application* [2000] NI 330.
11 See para **2.44**.
12 See written answer in House of Commons, HC Debs, vol 348, cos 222w–223w (12 April 2000).
13 Lord Chancellor's Department Press Notice 194/00, 5 June 2000.

6.18 [*Contd*] The Northern Ireland Assembly became operational on 2 December 1999 but was suspended by the Secretary of State on 11 February 2000 because of the lack of movement concerning the decommissioning of weapons on the part of Republican and Loyalist paramilitaries. On 12 February 2000 direct rule once more took effect in Northern Ireland, this time under the hastily enacted Northern Ireland Act 2000. Suspension of the Assembly was eventually ended on 30 May 2000.

6.21 [*Contd*] In exercise of its reserved powers to deal with the maintenance of public order and the functions of the Parades Commission for Northern Ireland, the Government seriously contemplated commencing the Human Rights Act 1998 in April 2000 for the specific purpose of allowing challenges to determinations of the Parades Commission under ss 8, 9 and 11 of the Public Processions (NI) Act 1998. The Northern Ireland Human Rights Commission advised the Government against introducing the Human Rights Act in this piecemeal fashion and the Government abandoned the idea.

8   NIA 1998, Sch 3, para 10. The Parades Commission was created by the Public Processions (NI) Act 1998.

6.24 [*Contd*] During the short initial life of the Northern Ireland Assembly (2 December 1999 to 11 February 2000), only four Bills were introduced and only one of them was enacted[2]. All of them, however, carried a Ministerial statement to the effect that they were within the legislative competence of the Assembly (and therefore compatible with the Convention). Since the re-establishment of the Assembly on 30 may 2000, a further 5 Bills have been introduced.

2   Financial Assistance for Political Parties Act 2000; Assembly Members' Pensions Bill (NIA Bill 1/99); Allowances to Members of the Assembly and Office Holders Bill (NIA Bill 2/99); Equality (Disability, etc) Bill (NIA Bill 4/99).

6.29 [*Contd*] Again, during the life of the Northern Ireland Assembly to date, the Presiding Officer (Lord Alderdice) has sent a copy of each of the Bills introduced to the Northern Ireland Human Rights Commission. The Commission has had to make substantive comment on only one of them.

6.31 [*Contd*] Rules of court have now been made to deal with the handling of devolution issues by various courts[4].

4   Magistrates' Courts (Devolution Issues) Rules (NI) 1999 (SR 1999/489); County Court (Amendment No 4) Rules (NI) 1999 (SR 1999/490); Crown Court (Amendment No 2) Rules (NI) 1999 (SR 1999/491); Criminal Appeal (Devolution Issues) Rules (NI) 1999 (SR 1999/492); Rules of the Supreme Court (NI) (Amendment No 3) 1999 (SR 1999/493).

6.41 [*Contd*] Although the text envisages the Human Rights Commission involving itself in court proceedings in only two types of situation, it is now clear that the Commission can also involve itself by applying to the court for permission – apparently to be granted under the common law power vesting in judges to hear whatever views they deem relevant to the questions at issue – to intervene in court proceedings as an interested third party. To date (by 14 August 2000) the Commission has sought such permission on five occasions (including a group of cases before the European Court of Human Rights[5]) and permission has been granted in each case[6]. In three of the four Northern Ireland cases the judge has permitted the Commission not just to make a written submission but also to attend court to answer questions about the submission, from either the judge or the parties to the dispute. However in the fourth case, *Re White's Application*[7], Lord Chief Justice Carswell refused permission to the Commission's counsel to make an oral submission. He said that he did not need to hear such oral submissions because there was no issue of sufficient consequence raised in the written submission which could not be adequately dealt with by counsel for one of the other parties. More generally he stated that leave to present oral argument should be given 'very sparingly'. After studying the written submission in the case before him, which drew upon the provisions of a range of international conventions, the Lord Chief Justice expressed the hope that 'if outside bodies wish in future to intervene in litigation or present written submissions, they will confine themselves strictly to relevant and apposite matters which directly address the issues before the court.'

5   See para **6.08** above.
6   These submissions are all available on the Commission's website at www.nihrc.org.
7   (18 May 2000, unreported). The case concerned a challenge to the representativeness of the Parades Commission, a body which has seven members, all of whom are male.

6.41A   The Commission has developed criteria to which it adheres when deciding whether to apply to intervene in a court case as an interested third party:

a) Do the proceedings relate to the law as it applies to Northern Ireland?
b) Is a rule or principle for the protection of human rights relevant to the proceedings?
c) Is the rule or principle one which relates to an area of work included in the Commission's Strategic Plan or to another human rights issue which could benefit from the Commission's attention?
d) Is there a possibility that if the Commission were to make a submission explaining the relevant rule or principle it might assist the court in coming to a conclusion on the matter?
e) Is it practicable for the Commission to make a submission in view of the time and resources available to prepare it?
f) Is intervention as a third party the most appropriate course of action for the Commission to take on this matter?

6.42   [*Contd*] As regards criteria for deciding when to grant assistance to individual applicants, these are already prescribed to some extent by s 70(2) of the Northern Ireland Act 1998. The Northern Ireland Human Rights Commission has refined these by (a) requiring all of them, not just one of them, to be satisfied in any particular case) and (b) setting out 'other special circumstances' for the purposes of s 70(2)(c). According to the Commission, special circumstances are those where:

a) it appears that the application relates to alleged non-compliance with a rule or principle for the protection of human rights based either in domestic law or in international standards, and

b) it appears that there is no other body in the circumstances which might be better placed to provide assistance to the applicant, and

c) it appears to be practicable for the Commission to provide assistance to the applicant having regard to the above criteria and to any other relevant criteria, eg the Commission's existing caseload or the Commission's resources, and

d) it appears that the application relates to an area of work included in the Commission's Strategic Plan or to another human rights issue which would benefit from the Commission's attention, and

e) it appears that this case is likely to have a significant impact on the protection of human rights (eg by affecting a large number of people or by addressing a serious violation of human rights).

6.43 [*Contd*] As regards its power to bring cases to court in its own name, the Northern Ireland Human Rights Commission has decided that it will do so if it believes that this is the most effective way of highlighting or remedying what the Commission believes to be a serious human rights abuse or a pattern of less serious human rights abuses.

6.45 [*Contd*] It is important to bear in mind a crucial difference in wording between the way in which s 75 of the Northern Ireland Act deals with equality of opportunity and good relations. In relation to the former it requires designated public authorities to have 'due regard' to the 'need' to promote it; in relation to good relations it requires such authorities to have 'regard' to the 'desirability' of promoting it.

6.46 [*Contd*] The Equality Commission for Northern Ireland issued Guidelines for the production of equality schemes in March 2000[4].

4   *Guide to the Statutory Duties*, Equality Commission for Northern Ireland, March 2000.

6.48 [*Contd*] A Designation Order was eventually made on 5 July 2000. It did not designate either the police bodies referred to in this paragraph or any of the further and higher education institutions in Northern Ireland. But the Police (NI) Bill, currently going through Parliament, makes provision for the new Police Service of Northern Ireland and the proposed Policing Board, to have designated status and the government has undertaken to include the educational establishments, and possibly other bodies (identified in submissions made by the Equity Commission for Northern Ireland and the Northern Ireland Human Rights Commission) in a subsequent designation Order. As of 23 May 2000, a Designation Order had still not been made. A draft of the Order existed but it did not mention either the police bodies referred to in this paragraph or any of the further and higher education institutions in Northern Ireland. The Equality Commission and others made representations to the Government about these omissions and as a result the Government announced (a) that it would extend the designation to the Police Service of Northern Ireland and the Policing Board once the legislation to implement the proposals made in the Patten Report had been enacted[2] and (b) that it would give further consideration to the inclusion of further and higher educational establishments in the category of designated authorities.

2   The Police (NI) Bill was introduced into the House of Commons on 16 May 2000.

6.49   [*Contd*] It seems clear that the NIA 1998, s 76 does not extend to indirect discrimination, but the same presumptions concerning the burden of proof apply as in other instances of alleged direct discrimination.

6.50   [*Contd*] The Equality Commission was appointed in September 1999. It comprises 20 members, including a Chief Commissioner and a Deputy Chief Commissioner. While the Equality Commission remains subject to the oversight of the Commissioner for Complaints in Northern Ireland, the Northern Ireland Human Rights Commission, being funded by the Northern Ireland Office and answerable to the Secretary of State and Parliament at Westminster, is subject to the oversight of the UK Parliamentary Commissioner for Administration[6]. From 25 April 2000, the same day as the Disability Rights Commission came into being in Great Britain, the Equality Commission for Northern Ireland acquired the power to grant assistance to individuals alleging discrimination under the Disability Discrimination Act 1995[7].

6   Parliamentary Commissioner Order 1999, SI 1999/227.
7   By virtue of the Equality (Disability, etc) (NI) Order 2000, SI 2000/1110. This was originally introduced as a Bill in the Northern Ireland Assembly, but the Assembly was suspended before the Bill could be enacted.

6.51

2   See Brice Dickson: 'The Human Rights Act and Northern Ireland' in M Hunt and R Singh *A Practitioner's Guide to the Impact of the Human Rights Act 1998*, ch 25 (due to be published in Autumn 2000). The area of law most likely to be affected is that of criminal law and procedure. Unfortunately no specific mention of Northern Ireland's criminal law and procedure is made in either N Richardson 'Criminal Law and Practice', in C Baker *Human Rights Act 1998: A Practitioner's Guide* (1998), pp 127–173, or in D Cheney, L Dickson, J Fitzpatrick and S Uglow *Criminal Justice and the Human Rights Act 1998* (1999).

Chapter 7

Wales

7.06

1   Section 107 was brought into force by the Government of Wales Act 1998 (Commencement No 4) Order 1999, SI 1999/782 with effect from 1 April 1999.

7.15   [*Contd*] A Practice Direction has been issued in respect of proceedings in England and Wales in the Court of Appeal (Civil and Criminal Divisions), the High Court, the Crown Court, the county courts and the magistrates' courts[1]. Rules have also been issued in respect of proceedings before the Judicial Committee[2].

1   Practice Direction (Supreme Court: Devolution) [1999] 1 WLR 1592.
2   The Judicial Committee (Devolution Issues) Rules Order 1999, SI 1999/665.

7.15A   In both civil and criminal proceedings the court may raise the question of whether a devolution issue arises to be considered of its own volition or where raised by the parties[1], and may give such directions as it considers appropriate to obtain clarification or additional information to determine that question[2]. If it determines that a devolution issue does arise the court must state what it is clearly and concisely[3] and order a devolution issue notice in the prescribed form to be given to the Attorney-General and the Assembly, unless already a party to the proceedings[4]. The devolution notice must specify the date (14 days after the issue date, or exceptionally longer by direction of the court) by which the Attorney-General and the Assembly must notify the court that he or it wishes to take part in the proceedings, so far as they relate to a devolution issue[5]. During that period the court may make such other orders as it thinks fit, including adjourning or staying the proceedings[6]. Where applicable, in criminal cases it must take into account whether it would involve delay which might extend beyond relevant custody time limits[7].

1   Paragraphs 5.1–5.2.
2   Paragraph 6.1.
3   Paragraph 6.3.
4   Paragraph 7.1. At the date of writing no devolution issue notices have been given.
5   Paragraph 7.5.
6   Paragraph 7.9(1).
7   Paragraph 7.9(2).

7.15B   If neither the Attorney-General nor the Assembly notifies the court within the specified time limit that he or it wishes to take part as a party, the proceedings should proceed immediately upon the expiry of that time[1]. If either wishes to participate, he or it must send a notice in the prescribed form to the court and other parties[2]. If either wishes to require the court to refer the matter to the Judicial Committee, he or it must as soon as practicable send to the court and other parties a notice in the prescribed form[3]. If the court is not required to refer the issue to the Judicial Committee the court will itself decide whether to refer it, before which it may hold a directions hearing or give written directions as to the making of submissions, and may decide, if its procedures permit, to make a decision on the basis of written submissions or have a hearing[4]. In exercising its discretion the court will have regard to all relevant circumstances including the importance of the devolution issue to the public in general and to the original parties, whether a decision on the devolution issue will be decisive of the matters in dispute between the parties, whether all relevant findings of fact have been made, and the delay (particularly in cases involving children and criminal cases) and additional costs that might be involved[5]. Provision is made for the form and procedure for references to the Judicial Committee[6], which should follow the procedure in the Judicial Committee (Devolution Issues) Rules[7]. If a reference is made the court will adjourn or stay the proceedings unless it otherwise orders[8].

1 Paragraph 7.10.
2 Paragraph 8.1.
3 Paragraph 8.3.
4 Paragraph 9.1–9.3.
5 Paragraph 9.4.
6 Paragraphs 10.1–10.4.
7 The Judicial Committee (Devolution Issues) Rules Order 1999, SI 1999/665.
8 Paragraph 11.

7.15C   In civil proceedings the devolution issue must be specified in sufficient detail in the pleadings[1]. If a party fails to do so and subsequently wishes to raise such an issue that party must seek the permission of the court[2]. If a devolution issue is raised during proceedings then a directions hearing must take place and the matter must be referred to a circuit judge (in county court actions) or High Court judge (in High Court actions) for determination and further directions[3].

1 Paragraphs 16.1–16.2.
2 Paragraph 16.4.
3 Paragraph 16.3.

7.15D   In respect of criminal proceedings in the Crown Court, if the defendant wishes to raise a devolution issue he should do so at the plea and directions hearing[1]. In the magistrates' court in both criminal and civil proceedings a defendant or party to a complaint or applicant for a licence wishing to raise a devolution issue should, wherever possible, give full particulars of the provisions relied upon by notice in writing as soon as possible after the 'not guilty' plea is entered or the complaint or application is made[2].

1 Paragraph 17.
2 Paragraph 18.1.

7.15E   Directions are provided for specific proceedings, namely judicial review proceedings, whereby applications may be lodged at the Crown Office in Cardiff if the application involves a devolution issue or judicial review of the Assembly or other Welsh public body[1], and family proceedings[2]. Provision is also made for the procedure for raising a devolution issue in any appeal to the Court of Appeal (both Civil and Criminal division)[3] and to the Crown Court[4].

1 Paragraphs 14.1–14.4.
2 Paragraphs 15.1–15.8.
3 Paragraph 19.
4 Paragraph 20.

7.15F The GWA provides for equal treatment of the Welsh and English languages[1], including the requirement that all subordinate legislation be prepared in English and Welsh (except where the responsible Assembly Secretary considers it would be inappropriate or not reasonably practicable)[2], and both texts are to be treated as being of equal standing[3]. Accordingly, where a party wishes to put forward a contention in relation to a devolution issue that requires comparison of the Welsh and English texts of any Assembly subordinate legislation, the Practice Direction provides for the appointment, where necessary, of a Welsh speaking judicial assessor to assist the court[4].

1   Section 47(1), following upon the Welsh Language Act 1993. See *Williams v Cowell* [2000] 1 WLR 187 (refusal by Employment Appeal Tribunal to order appeal to be heard in Wales was not contrary to the principle of equality of the Welsh language, nor in conflict with either art 6 (read with art 14) or art 10).
2   Section 66(4).
3   Section 122.
4   Paragraph 12.

Chapter 8

International Human Rights Codes and United Kingdom Law

8.09 [*Contd*] The General Comments and General Recommendations of the UN treaty-based bodies are readily available on the Internet through the Human Rights section of www.un.org.org. The Human Rights Committee has made the following General Comments, see para **8.10** below.

8.10 [*Contd*] Table of Contents of General Comments on the ICCPR.

No of Report	Subject Matter	Year Adopted
27[1]	Freedom of Movement	1999
28	Equality of rights between men and women	2000

1   Reprinted in (2000) 7 IHRR 1.

8.12   Ninety-five states, of which 14 are members of the European Union, have granted the right of individual petition under the First Optional Protocol to the ICCPR. The UK Government has:

'no present plans to grant new rights of petition under any United Nations human rights treaty. This reflects the outcome of a thorough review of our obligations under international human rights treaties in March 1999. We will review the position again when the Human Rights Act 1998 has been implemented and is properly bedded down'[1].

Until this bedding-down process is complete, the Government considers that preparing for the right of individual petition and responding to any complaints that may be brought under this procedure, is 'likely to divert resources from implementing the HRA 1998'[2].

1   612 HL Official Report (5th series) (12 April 2000), WA 49.
2   612 HL Official Report (5th series), (2 May 2000), WA 156.

8.18A   In ratifying the ICCPR, the UK Government expressed a reservat on with regard to the requirement contained in art 20 to prohibit by law the advocacy of religious hatred. It interpreted art 20 consistently with art 19 (free expression) and reserved the right not to introduce any further legislation on incitement to religious hatred[1]. The Government has no immediate plans to lift this reservation. Incitement to racial hatred is an offence under Part III of the Public Order Act 1986. For the purposes of this offence, 'racial hatred' if defined as hatred against a group of persons in Great Britain defined by reference to colour, race, nationality (including citizenship) or ethnic or national origins. There is no specific provision in British law that and incitement to religious hatred, in contrast to the position in Northern Ireland, where the Public Order (Northern Ireland) Order 1987 does make it an offence to incite hatred against a group of persons defined by religious belief. The Government has justified this approach by citing the particular circumstances of Northern Ireland which 'require particular measures which it may not be suitable to apply to the United Kingdom', while emphasising that the issue of incitement to religious hatred is being kept under review[2].

1   See Jepson, P 'Tackling Religious Terminology that Stirs up Religious Hatred', [1999] NLJ 554.
2   610 HL Official Report (5th Series) (17 May 2000), WA 21.

8.18B   The absence of legislation on religious discrimination in general outside of Northern Ireland is also under review. 'The Government are listening to the concerns of minority faith communities about the issues of religious discrimination and the case for it to be made subject to the law. The issue raises many difficult, sensitive and complex questions'. The Government has commissioned a team from the University of Derby to conduct research and to assess the current scale and nature of religious discrimination. The results, due in Autumn 2000, 'will help to inform our thinking about the appropriate response regarding religious discrimination and incitement of religious hatred'[1].

1   612 HL Official Report (5th Series) (12 April 2000), WA 50.

8.21   The Government has decided to maintain reservations on art 10(2)(b) and (3) of the ICCPR and art 37(c) of the UN Convention on the Rights of the Child (which prohibit mixing young offenders and adult prisoners). The Government agrees in principle that young prisoners should be held separately from adults. It has provided £51 million to enable the Prison Service to create a distinct facility for young men under 18 years old. However, there continues to be a small number of young men 'whose particular circumstances mean that they are best temporarily held in adult prisons, for example, because of distance from court' or for reasons of security, medical requirements or the availability of specialist facilities[1]. The Government has decided that 'young women aged 15–16 should be placed in non-Prison Service accommodation, and those aged 17 years as spaces become available. In the interim, 17 year-olds on remand will continue to share facilities with adults due to their small numbers, and those sentenced with other young women under 21 in enhanced young offender units in women's prisons'[2]. It is estimated that this process will take two years to complete[3].

1   613 HL Official Report (5th series) (17 May 2000), WA 20.
2   612 HL Official Report (5th series) (12 April 2000), WA 49.
3   613 HL Official Report (5th series) (17 May 2000), WA 21.

8.31   The CERD has made the following General Recommendations:

No of Report	Subject Matter	Year Adopted
XXIII	Rights of indigenous peoples	1997
XXIV	Article 1	1999
XXV	Gender related dimensions of racial discrimination	2000

8.42 The Committee on the Elimination of Discrimination Against Women has made the following General Recommendations:

No of Report	Subject Matter	Year Adopted
24	Women's Health	1999

8.42A On 15 October 1999, a new Optional Protocol to CEDAW was adopted and opened for signature and ratification by the member states of the UN[1]. This Protocol gives the Committee on the Elimination of Discrimination Against Women competence to receive and consider communications submitted by individuals, or groups of individuals, claiming to be victims of a violation of any of the rights set forth in CEDAW. The UK has declined to sign the Optional Protocol, but will review its position 'once the Human Rights Act has bedded in'[2].

1   UN Resolution A/RES/54/4. The text of the Optional Protocol can be found in (2000) 7 IHRR 294.
2   611 HL Official Report (5th series) (20 March 2000) WA 1.

8.58 [*Contd*] The Committee Against Torture has made one General Comment, namely the General Comment on the implementation of art 3 of the Convention in the context of art 22[1].

1   See (1999) 6 IHRR 599.

8.89 The Committee on Economic, Social and Cultural Rights has made the following General Comments on the ICESCR:

No of Report	Subject Matter	Year Adopted
8	The relationship between economic sanctions and respect for economic, social and cultural rights	1997
9	The domestic application of the Covenant	1998
10	The role of national human rights in the protection of economic, social and cultural rights	1998
11	Plans of action for primary education	1999
12	The right to adequate food	1999
13	The right to education	1999

APPENDIX 3

Human Rights Act 1998 Materials and Commentary

Procedure Rules and Practice Directions

In framing the HRA the Government's intention was to avoid having to create new procedures, courts and remedies, wherever possible, in the belief that the statutory scheme should allow for most situations. The areas where substantive new provisions are required and made are limited to the following:

Section 2: citation of Strasbourg jurisprudence;
Section 5: notification of the Crown where the court is considering making a declaration of incompatibility;
Section 7: procedures for dealing with claims brought under the HRA alone rather than in existing proceedings; and
Section 9: joining the Crown to proceedings involving a claim for damages in respect of a judicial act, and ensuring that such proceedings are heard in the appropriate court.
Civil Procedure Rules and Practice Directions for the civil courts, Family Procedure Rules and Practice Directions for the family courts and Criminal Appeal (Amendment) Rules for criminal proceedings in England and Wales up to and including the Court of Appeal come into force on 2 October 2000, with the implementation of the main provisions of the HRA.

Many other tribunals do not have specific power to make formal practice directions but are governed by rules allowing them to regulate their own proceedings, including the circulation of informal guidance, and the Lord Chancellor's Department has invited them to do so.

Under the Family and Civil Procedure Practice Directions, any party seeking to rely on any provision of or right arising under the HRA, or who is seeking a remedy under that Act must state this and give precise details of the ECHR right infringed, details of the Infringement and specify the relief sought. This requirement applies in all situations. If a declaration of incompatibility is sought, or damages in respect of a judicial act to which section 9 (3) of the HRA applies, or the claim is based on such a judicial act, then precise details of the alleged incompatibility or judicial act are required.

Item 3 of the Additions to Civil Procedure Practice Directions, to be inserted in the practice direction to CPR Part 16 (Statements of case):

'**Human Rights**
16.1 A party who seeks to rely on any provision of or right arising under the Human Rights Act 1998 or seeks a remedy available under that Act—
    (1) must state that fact in his statement of case; and

(2)　must in his statement of case—
- (a)　give precise details of the Convention right which its is alleged has been infringed and details of the alleged infringement;
- (b)　specify the relief sought;
- (c)　state if the relief sought includes—
  - (i)　a declaration of incompatibility in accordance with section 4 of that Act, or
  - (ii)　damages in respect of a judicial act to which section 9(3) of that Act applies;
- (d)　where the relief sought includes a declaration of incompatibility in accordance with section 4 of that Act, give precise details of the legislative provision alleged to be incompatible and details of the alleged incompatibility;
- (e)　where the claim is founded on a finding of unlawfulness by another court or tribunal, give details of the finding; and
- (f)　where the claim is founded on a judicial act which is alleged to have infringed a Convention right of the party as provided by section 9 of the Human Rights Act 1998, the judicial act complained of and the court or tribunal which is alleged to have made it.

(The practice direction to Part 19 provides for notice to be given and parties joined in the circumstances referred to in (c), (d) and (f))

16.2　A party who seeks to amend his statement of case to include the matters referred to in paragraph 16.1 must, unless the court orders otherwise, do so as soon as possible. (Part 17 provides for the amendment of a statement of case).'

Item 10a of the Additions to Civil Procedure Practice Directions, to be inserted in the practice direction to CPR Part 52 (Appeals):

'Human Rights

5.1A Where the appellant is seeking to rely on any issue under the Human Rights Act 1998, or seeks a remedy available under that Act, for the first time in an appeal he must include in his appeal notice the information required by paragraph 16.1 of the practice direction to CPR Part 16. Paragraph 16.2 of that practice direction also applies as if references to statement of case were to appeal notice.

5.1B CPR rule 19.4A and the practice direction supplementing it shall apply as if references to the case management conference were to the application for permission to appeal.

(The practice direction to Part 19 provides for notice to be given and parties joined in certain circumstances to which this paragraph applies)'.

Item 10b of the Additions to Civil Procedure Practice Directions, to be inserted in the practice direction to CPR Part 52 (Appeals):

'**7.3A**　Paragraphs 5.1A and 5.1B of this practice direction also apply to a respondent and a respondent's notice'.

SECTION 2 – CITATION OF AUTHORITIES

Instead of making rules under Section 2(2), the Government decided that it would be more appropriate not to specify in detail what can be cited as Strasbourg jurisprudence. This is a different approach from that originally set out in the CPR Consultation Paper published by the Lord Chancellor's Department in March

2000, which set out in a proposed practice direction a list of preferred texts of Strasbourg jurisprudence. The approach finally adopted in the new Practice Directions has the advantage of flexibility, especially given the proliferation of new law reports in this new area of law.

Item 8 of the Additions to Civil Procedure Practice Directions, to be inserted in the first practice direction to CPR Part 39 (Hearings):

'**Citation of Authorities**
Human Rights
8.1 If it is necessary for a party to give evidence at a hearing of an authority referred to in section 2 of the Human Rights Act 1998—
    (1)   the authority to be cited should be an authoritative and complete report; and
    (2)   the party must give to the court and any other party a list of the authorities he intends to cite and copies of the reports not less than three days before the hearing.
(Section 2(1) of the Human Rights Act 1998 requires the court to take into account the authorities listed there)
    (3)   Copies of the complete original texts issued by the European Court and Commission either paper based or from the Court's judgment database (HUDOC), which is available on the Internet, may be used'.

To be included in the new family proceedings practice direction:

'CITATION OF AUTHORITIES
2.   When an authority referred to in section 2 of the Human Rights Act 1998 ('the Act') is to be cited at a hearing:
    (a)   the authority to be cited shall be an authoritative and complete report;
    (b)   the court must be provided with a list of authorities it is intended to cite and copies of the reports—
        (i)   in cases to which the President's Direction (Court Bundles) dated 10th March 2000 applies, as part of the bundle;
        (ii)   otherwise, not less than 2 clear days before the hearing, and
    (c)   copies of the complete original texts issued by the European Court and Commission, either paper based or from the Court's judgment database (HUDOC), which is available on the Internet, may be used.

SECTIONS 4 AND 5 – DECLARATIONS OF INCOMPATIBILITY

The HRA provides that, so far as it is possible to do so, primary (and subordinate) legislation must be read and given effect in a way that is compatible with the Convention rights. Where, in spite of its efforts to read a provision of primary legislation compatibly, a Court is satisfied that it is incompatible with a Convention right, it may, if it is a court listed in section 4(5), make a declaration of incompatibility. The courts listed in section 4(5) are the House of Lords, the Judicial Committee of the Privy Council, the Courts-Martial Appeal Court, in Scotland the High Court of Judiciary sitting otherwise than as a trial court or the Court of Session, or in England, Wales and Northern Ireland the High Court or the Court of Appeal. The new Civil Procedure Rules, Practice Directions, and Family Law Practice directions confine the hearing and determination of claims of incompatibility to High Court judges, excluding deputy High Court judges, Masters or District Judges. A new CPR Rule 30.3 (2) (g) provides for a transfer to the High Court where the question of the making of a declaration of incompatibility has arisen, and the Civil Procedure Practice Directions also provide that a transfer on this basis should only be made 'where there is a real prospect that a declaration of incompatibility will be made'.

New CPR Rule 30.3 (2) (g):
   '(g)   whether the making of a declaration of incompatibility under section 4 of the Human Rights Act 1998 has arisen or may arise'.

Item 1a to be inserted in Civil Procedure Practice Direction 2B to CPR Part 2 (first section for the High Court):

'Human Rights
  8A A deputy High Court Judge, a Master or District Judge may not try—
     (1) a case in a claim made in respect of a judicial act under the Human Rights Act 1998, or
     (2) a claim for a declaration of incompatibility in accordance with section 4 of the Human Rights Act 1998'.

Item 7 of the additions to the Civil Procedure Practice Directions, to be added to the practice direction to CPR Part 30:

'Transfer on the criterion in rule 30.3(2)(g)
A transfer should only be made on the basis of the criterion in rule 30.3(2)(g) where there is a real prospect that a declaration of incompatibility will be made'.

To be added to the Family Law Practice directions:

'Allocation to judges
  3   (1)   The hearing and determination of the following will be confined to a High Court Judge:
     (a) a claim for a declaration of incompatibility under section 4 of the Act; or
     (b) an issue which may lead to the court considering making such a declaration'.

After section 4, Section 5(1) then provides that 'where a Court is considering whether to make declaration of incompatibility, the Crown is entitled to notice in accordance with rules of court'. Provision is made to give effect to the intention of the legislation that the Crown should be notified at the earliest time, rather than just before a declaration is made. However, notice is not required to be given any earlier; for example, if a party seeks the remedy in a claim form.

The provision gives the Crown the opportunity, if it wishes, to make any relevant arguments to the Court before it decides to make a declaration. While there is a requirement for the Crown to be notified, there is no requirement for the Crown to intervene. This will depend upon the circumstances of the case.

Under Section 5(1), it will be the court that provides notice to the Crown once it begins to consider making a declaration of incompatibility, rather than the parties. This is because it is the court that is considering making the declaration and it is the court that will be best placed to provide useful information to the Crown to enable it to determine whether it wishes to be joined as a party. This approach gives the court prime responsibility for managing the case, as encouraged in the Civil Procedure Rules.

The civil, family and criminal appeal rules and practice directions therefore stipulate that notice is to be given by the Court itself in writing and should be sent to the person named in the list published by HM Treasury under Section 17 of the Crown Proceedings Act 1947. The notice should contain sufficient details to identify the claim, the parties to the claim, the court, the Convention rights under consideration and a short statement of the issues which have led to the Court considering making a declaration of incompatibility.

Section 5(3) provides that notice by the Crown under Section 5(2) that it wishes to take up its entitlement to be joined can be given at any time during the proceedings. Once the court gives notice, however, the court will need to allow the Crown a minimum period of time to determine whether it wishes to be joined. A balance needs to be struck here between, on the one hand, affording the Crown sufficient time to make a reasoned decision on whether it wishes to be joined and, on the other, not delaying the case. The Crown is allowed 21 days in the first instance to state whether it wished to be joined as a party, unless the circumstances of the case mean that the Court orders otherwise. The Crown is able to apply, if necessary, for an extension of the time limit.

Where the Minister has nominated a person to be joined as a party the notice must be accompanied by the written nomination. Notice should be given to the relevant Government Department (or if none, or if the court is uncertain which is the relevant department, the Attorney General) even where the Crown is already party to the proceedings in some other capacity. This is to ensure that the specific issue of the fact that the Court is considering making a declaration of incompatibility is considered appropriately by the Crown.

New CPR Rule 19.4A, to be inserted after CPR rule 19.4, in Part 19 (Parties and Group Litigation):

'Human Rights
Section 4 of the Human Rights Act 1998
19.4A   (1)   The court may not make a declaration of incompatibility in accordance with section 4 of the Human Rights Act 1998 unless 21 days' notice, or such other period of notice as the court directs, has been given to the Crown.
            (2)   Where notice has been given to the Crown a Minister, or other person permitted by that Act, shall be joined as a party on giving notice to the court.
(Only courts specified in section 4 of the Human Rights Act 1998 can make a declaration of incompatibility)

CPR Rule 19.4 (3) — (4) concerns claims under sections 7 (1) (a) and 9 (3) of the HRA for damages in respect of judicial acts, and are reproduced below'.

Item 4 of the Additions to Civil Procedure Practice Directions, to be inserted in the first practice direction to CPR Part 19 (Parties and Group Litigation):

'Human Rights, Joining the Crown
Section 4 of the Human Rights Act 1998
6.1   Where a party has included in his statement of case—

(1)   a claim for a declaration of incompatibility in accordance with section 4 of the Human Rights Act 1998, or

(2)   an issue for the court to decide which may lead to the court considering making a declaration,

then the court may at any time consider whether notice should be given to the Crown as required by that Act and give directions for the content and service of the notice.   The rule allows a period of 21 days before the court will make the declaration but the court may vary this period of time.

6.2   The court will normally consider the issues and give the directions referred to in paragraph 6.1 at the case management conference.

6.3   Where a party amends his statement of case to include any matter referred to in paragraph 6.1, then the court will consider whether notice should be given to the Crown and give directions for the content and service of the notice.

(The practice direction to CPR Part 16 requires a party to include issues under the Human Rights Act 1998 in his statement of case).

6.4   (1)   The notice given under rule 19.4A must be served on the person named in the list published under s. 17 of the Crown Proceedings Act 1947.

(The list, made by the Minister for the Civil Service, is annexed to this practice direction).

(2)   The notice will be in the form directed by the court but will normally include the directions given by the court and all the statements of case in the claim. The notice will also be served on all the parties.

(3)   The court may require the parties to assist in the preparation of the notice.

(4)   In the circumstances described in the National Assembly for Wales (Transfer of Functions)(No. 2) Order 2000 the notice must also be served on the National Assembly for Wales.

(Section 5(3) of the Human Rights Act 1998 provides that the Crown may give notice that it intends to become a party at any stage in the proceedings once notice has been given).

Unless the court orders otherwise, the Minister or other person permitted by the Human Rights Act 1998 to be joined as a party must, if he wishes to be joined, give notice of his intention to be joined as a party to the court and every other party. Where the Minister has nominated a person to be joined as a party the notice must be accompanied by the written nomination.

(Section 5(2)(a) of the Human Rights Act 1998 permits a person nominated by a Minister of the Crown to be joined as a party. The nomination may be signed on behalf of the Minister)'.

Part 6.6 of this Practice Direction concerns claims under sections 7 (1) (a) and 9 (3) of the HRA for damages in respect of judicial acts, and is reproduced below:

The Criminal Appeal (Amendment) Rules 2000 provide that the Criminal Appeal Rules 1968 are to be amended as follows:

'Amendment of Criminal Appeal Rules 1968

"2.   The Criminal Appeal Rules 1968[1] shall be amended as follows—

(a)   in rule 2, after paragraph (2)(a) there shall be inserted—

'(aa) A notice of the grounds of appeal or application set out in Form 3 shall include notice—

(i)   of any application to be made to the court for a declaration of incompatibility under section 4 of the Human Rights Act 1998; or

(ii)   of any issue for the court to decide which may lead to the court making such a declaration .

(ab) Where the grounds of appeal or application include notice in accordance with paragraph (aa) above, a copy of the notice shall be served on the prosecutor by the appellant."

(b)   after rule 14 there shall be inserted—

"Human Rights Act

    14A.(1)The court shall not consider making a declaration of incompatibility under section 4 of the Human Rights Act 1998 unless it has given written notice to the Crown.

    (2)   Where notice has been given to the Crown, a Minister, or other person entitled under or required by the Human Rights Act 1998 to be joined as a party, shall be so joined on giving written notice to the court.

    (3)   A notice given under paragraph (1) above shall be given to—

        (a)   the person named in the list published under section 17(1) of the Crown Proceedings Act 1947[2]; or

        (b)   in the case of doubt as to whether any and if so which of those departments is appropriate, the Treasury Solicitor.

    (4)   A notice given under paragraph (1) above, shall provide an outline of the issues in the case and specify—

        (a)   the prosecutor and appellant;

        (b)   the date, judge and court of the trial in the proceedings from which the appeal lies;

        (c)   the provision of primary legislation and the Convention right under question.

    (5)   Any consideration of whether a declaration of incompatibility should be made, shall be adjourned for—

        (a)   21 days from the date of the notice given under paragraph (1) above; or

        (b)   such other period (specified in the notice), as the court shall allow in order that the relevant Minister or other person, may seek to be joined and prepare his case.

    (6)   Unless the court otherwise directs, the Minister or other person entitled under or required by the Human Rights Act 1998 to be joined as a party shall, if he is to be joined, give written notice to the court and every other party.

    (7)   Where a Minister of the Crown has nominated a person to be joined as a party by virtue of section 5(2)(a) of the Human Rights Act 1998, a notice under paragraph (6) above shall be accompanied by a written nomination signed by or on behalf of the Minister."

(c)   in rule 15 after paragraph (1)(d) there shall be inserted—

    "(e) in the case of a declaration of incompatibility under section 4 of the Human Rights Act 1998, the declaration shall be served on—

        (i)   all of the parties to the proceedings; and

        (ii)   where a Minister of the Crown has not been joined as a party, the Crown (in accordance with rule 14A(3) above).'''.

1   SI 1968/1262. Rule 2 was amended by SIs 1987/1977 and 1989/1102.
2   1947 c 44.

New FPR Rule 10.26, to be inserted after FPR rule 10.25:

'Human Rights Act 1998

10.26   (1)   In this rule—

    'originating document' means a petition, application, originating application, originating summons or other originating process;

    'answer' means an answer or other document filed or served by a party in reply to an originating document (but not an acknowledgement of service);

    'Convention right' has the same meaning as in the Human Rights Act 1998[1];

    'declaration of incompatibility' means a declaration of incompatibility under section 4 of the Human Rights Act 1998.

(2) A party who seeks to rely on any provision of or right arising under the Human Rights Act 1998 or seeks a remedy available under that Act—

    (a) shall state that fact in his originating document or (as the case may be) answer; and

    (b) shall in his originating document or (as the case may be) answer—

        (i) give precise details of the Convention right which it is alleged has been infringed and details of the alleged infringement;

        (ii) specify the relief sought;

        (iii) state if the relief sought includes a declaration of incompatibility.

(3) A party who seeks to amend his originating document or (as the case may be) answer to include the matters referred to in paragraph (2) shall, unless the court orders otherwise, do so as soon as possible and in any event not less than 28 days before the hearing.

(4) The court shall not make a declaration of incompatibility unless 21 days' notice, or such other period of notice as the court directs, has been given to the Crown.

(5) Where notice has been given to the Crown a Minister, or other person permitted by the Human Rights Act 1998, shall be joined as a party on giving notice to the court.

(6) Where a party has included in his originating document or (as the case may be) answer:

    (a) a claim for a declaration of incompatibility, or

    (b) an issue for the court to decide which may lead to the court considering making a declaration of incompatibility,

then the court may at any time consider whether notice should be given to the Crown as required by the Human Rights Act 1998 and give directions for the content and service of the notice.

(7) In the case of an appeal for which permission to appeal is required, the court shall, unless it decides that it is appropriate to do so at another stage in the proceedings, consider the issues and give the directions referred to in paragraph (6) when deciding whether to give such permission.

(8) If paragraph (7) does not apply, and a hearing for directions would, but for this rule, be held, the court shall, unless it decides that it is appropriate to do so at another stage in the proceedings, consider the issues and give the directions referred to in paragraph (6) at the hearing for directions.

(9) If neither paragraph (7) nor paragraph (8) applies, the court shall consider the issues and give the directions referred to in paragraph (6) when it considers it appropriate to do so, and may fix a hearing for this purpose.

(10) Where a party amends his originating document or (as the case may be) answer to include any matter referred to in paragraph (6)(a), then the court will consider whether notice should be given to the Crown and give directions for the content and service of the notice.

(11) In paragraphs (12) to (16), 'notice' means the notice given under paragraph (4).

(12) The notice shall be served on the person named in the list published under section 17 of the Crown Proceedings Act 1947.

(13) The notice shall be in the form directed by the court.

(14) Unless the court orders otherwise, the notice shall be accompanied by the directions given by the court and the originating document and any answers in the proceedings.

(15) Copies of the notice shall be served on all the parties.

(16) The court may require the parties to assist in the preparation of the notice.

(17) Unless the court orders otherwise, the Minister or other person permitted by the Human Rights Act 1998 to be joined as a party shall, if he wishes to be joined, give notice of his intention to be joined as a party to the court and every other party, and where the Minister has nominated a person to be joined as a party the notice must be accompanied by the written nomination'.

1   1998 c 42.

FPR Rule 10.26 (18) - (21) concerns claims under sections 7 (1) (a) and 9 (3) of the HRA for damages in respect of judicial acts, and is reproduced below:

FPR Rule 10.26 (22) is also reproduced below, and provides that on any application or appeal concerning a committal order, a refusal to grant habeas corpus or a secure accommodation order made under section 25 of the Act of 1989, if the court ordering the release of the person concludes that his Convention rights have been infringed by the making of the order to which the application or appeal relates, the judgment or order should state this. However, if the court does not do so, that failure will not prevent another court from deciding the matter.

SECTION 7 – CLAIMS AGAINST A PUBLIC AUTHORITY WHICH HAS ACTED OR IS TO ACT CONTRARY TO SECTION 6

A free-standing case under Section 7(1)(a) of the Act will be brought in the following ways-
using the existing judicial review procedures;

>   in the county court or in the High Court where a claim for damages is made (unless this is associated with a claim for judicial review). The normal jurisdictional limits apply;

>   in the county court or in the High Court following a finding of unlawfulness under Section 7(1)(b) in some other court or tribunal which did not have the power to award damages or compensation. This covers, for example, actions in respect of a claim for damages in a criminal case arising out of a ruling by a Magistrates' Court or the Crown Court that the prosecution had acted unlawfully. The normal criteria for determining whether a civil case should be started in a county court or the High Court again apply. The person seeking a civil remedy will be able to rely upon the finding of unlawfulness in the other court as prima facie evidence that the defendant authority acted unlawfully. The previous finding of unlawfulness (even if it resulted from a collateral challenge in the earlier proceedings) will be treated, by analogy, in the same way that Section 11 of the Civil Evidence Act 1968 c.64 treats a conviction for the purpose of civil proceedings. It will be open to the defendant to refute the finding on grounds of fact or law using the authority under paragraph 4 of Schedule 1 to the Civil Procedure Act 1997.

Section 7(11) of the HRA enables Ministers to make rules for individual tribunals to ensure that they can provide appropriate relief or remedies in relation to an act of a public authority, which is unlawful under Section 6(1) of the HRA. It was thought that rules would be required in this respect for the Immigration Appellate Authorities but the position has been resolved here by the Immigration and Asylum Act 1999. No other tribunals requiring rules to this effect have yet been identified so there is no intention at this stage to draft rules under Section 7(11).

SECTION 9 – CLAIMS UNDER SECTION 7(1)(A) FOR JUDICIAL ACTS

Section 9 applies to proceedings under Section 7(1) (a) in respect of judicial acts. The Rules and Practice Directions that apply here are designed to ensure that:

a   Claims for damages based on allegations of the breach of Convention rights as a consequence of judicial acts are determined in the appropriate court, and

b   The Lord Chancellor can be joined to proceedings at a resource efficient stage that is convenient for all the parties involved.

The CPR Consultation Paper originally proposed that where a committal order made by a District Judge was appealed on the grounds that it breached Article 5, the matter could be transferred to the Crown Office List. This approach was adopted to direct these issues to the Divisional Court of the High Court, so that the novel and complex issues surrounding Article 5 unlawful detention fall to the senior judiciary to consider. It can therefore play a supervisory role during the early stages of incorporation, thus ensuring that consistent and authoritative principles are established in relation to Article 5 unlawful detention and the quantum of Article 5(5) damages. The new CPR Rules and Practice Directions now provide that a claim under section 7(1) (a) of the HRA in respect of a judicial act may be brought only in the High Court. If a claim for damages in the a notice of appeal, then it will be dealt with according to the normal rules governing where that appeal is heard.

This ensures High Court scrutiny of judicial act claims, and makes it clear that that having being released on appeal a claimant can mount a claim under section 7(1)(a) (including a claim under section 9 (3) for Article 5 damages). The CPR Practice Directions signpost the possibility that Parliament may direct some compensation claims to particular tribunals.

The new CPR Rules also make it clear that where a claim for a remedy under section 7 in respect of a judicial act is based on a finding by a court or tribunal that the claimant's Convention rights have been infringed, the court hearing the claim may proceed on the basis of the other court or tribunal's finding of an infringement. It is not obliged to do so however, and may reach its own conclusion in the light of the original finding and the evidence heard by the other court or tribunal. The CPR Practice Directions and the new FPR Rules provide that where a person is released on an application on appeal concerning a committal order, a refusal to grant habeas corpus or a secure accommodation order under section 25 of the Children's Act 1989, the court must state whether the original order infringed that person's Convention rights. If it does not do so, another court is not precluded from deciding the matter. This will therefore ensure that it will be usually clear whether the applicant is entitled to compensation, or whether their detention was quashed on grounds other than Article 5 of the Convention, as well as ensuring that the determination of many HRA claims can be focussed in the High Court.

Additions are also made to practice directions applying to civil and family courts, providing for a notice procedure as required by section 9(4). Section 9(4) requires that, for an award to be made under Section 9(3), the appropriate person must be joined to the proceedings (if not already a party). The practice direction provides that an applicant must state on the notice of appeal / application for judicial review if (s)he is seeking damages in respect of a judicial act. The Lord Chancellor should be notified at this stage, except where the judicial act is of a Court-Martial, where the appropriate authority is the Secretary of State for Defence. The authority then has 21 days to indicate whether he wishes to be joined from the outset, either to contest the substance of the claim, or to make representations on the quantum of damages. Otherwise he will be joined for the purposes of Section 9(4) if and when a finding of a breach is made.

New CPR Rule 7.11, to be inserted after CPR rule 7.10:

'Human Rights
7.11(1)   A claim under section 7(1)(a) of the Human Rights Act 1998[1] in respect of a judicial act may be brought only in the High Court.
(2)   Any other claim under section 7(1)(a) of that Act may be brought in any court."

1   1998 c 42.

New CPR 19.4A, to be inserted after CPR rule 19.4, along with the provisions noted above for giving notice to the Crown where the court is considering making a declaration of incompatibility:

'Human Rights
19.4A   (after the notice provisions for a declaration of incompatibility)
Section 9 of the Human Rights Act 1998
(3)   Where a claim is made under that Act for damages in respect of a judicial act –
    (a)   that claim must be set out in the statement of case or the appeal notice; and
    (b)   notice must be given to the Crown.
(4)   Where paragraph (3) applies and the appropriate person has not applied to be joined as a party within 21 days, or such other period as the court directs, after the notice is served, the court may join the appropriate person as a party.
(A practice direction makes provision for these notices)'.

New CPR Rule 33.9:

'Human Rights
33.9 (1)   This rule applies where a claim is—
    (a)   for a remedy under section 7 of the Human Rights Act 1998 in respect of a judicial act which is alleged to have infringed the claimant's Article 5 Convention rights; and
    (b)   based on a finding by a court or tribunal that the claimant's Convention rights have been infringed.
(2)   The court hearing the claim—
    (a)   may proceed on the basis of the finding of that other court or tribunal that there has been an infringement but it is not required to do so, and
    (b)   may reach its own conclusion in the light of that finding and of the evidence heard by that other court or tribunal.'.

Item 1a to be inserted in Civil Procedure Practice Direction 2B to CPR Part 2 (first section for the High Court):

'Human Rights
8A   A deputy High Court Judge, a Master or District Judge may not try—

(1) a case in a claim made in respect of a judicial act under the Human Rights Act 1998, or

(2) a claim for a declaration of incompatibility in accordance with section 4 of the Human Rights Act 1998'.

Item 1b of the additions to the civil procedure practice directions, to be inserted in Practice Direction 2B to CPR Part 2 (second section for county courts):

'Human Rights

15 A District Judge or Recorder may not try a case in a claim made in respect of a judicial act under the Human Rights Act 1998'.

Item 2 of the additions to the civil procedure practice directions, to be inserted in the practice direction to CPR Part 7 (How to start a claim):

'**6.5**   (1)   The normal rules apply in deciding in which court and specialist list a claim that includes issues under the Human Rights Act 1998 should be started. They also apply in deciding which procedure to use to start the claim; this Part or CPR Part 8 or CPR Part 54 (judicial review).

(2) The exception is a claim for damages in respect of a judicial act, which should be commenced in the High Court. If the claim is made in a notice of appeal then it will be dealt with according to the normal rules governing where that appeal is heard.

(A county court cannot make a declaration of incompatibility in accordance with section 4 of the Human Rights Act 1998. Legislation may direct that such a claim is to be brought before a specified tribunal)'.

Item 4 of the additions to the civil procedure practice directions, to be inserted in the practice direction to CPR Part 19 (Parties and Group Litigation). This provides both for the procedure for the giving of notice where a declaration of incompatibility is possible, and for the giving of notice where a claim is made for damages in respect of a judicial act:

'Human Rights, Joining the Crown

Sections 6.1 to 6.5 relate to the declaration of incompatibility, and are reproduced above.

Section 9 of the Human Rights Act 1998

6.6 (1)   The procedure in paragraphs 6.1 to 6.5 also applies where a claim is made under sections 7(1)(a) and 9(3) of the Human Rights Act 1998 for damages in respect of a judicial act.

(2) Notice must be given to the Lord Chancellor and should be served on the Treasury Solicitor on his behalf, except where the judicial act is of a Court-Martial when the appropriate person is the Secretary of State for Defence and the notice must be served on the Treasury Solicitor on his behalf.

(3) The notice will also give details of the judicial act, which is the subject of the claim for damages, and of the court or tribunal that made it.

(Section 9(4) of the Human Rights Act 1998 provides that no award of damages may be made against the Crown as provided for in section 9(3) unless the appropriate party is joined in the proceedings. The appropriate person is the Minister responsible for the court concerned or a person or department nominated by him (section 9(5) of the Act)).

The following additions to Civil Procedure Practice Directions are also relevant to the procedure for joining the Crown in cases involving judicial acts.

Item 5 of the additions to the civil procedure practice directions, to be inserted at the end of the list in the practice direction to Part 28 paragraph 1.2:

'Rule 19.4A and the practice direction supplementing it on joining the Crown in certain cases raising Convention rights issues'.

Item 6 of the additions to the civil procedure practice directions, to be added in the practice direction to Part 29 to the end of paragraph 1.2

', and Rule 19.4A and the practice direction supplementing it on joining the Crown in certain cases raising Convention rights issues'.

Item 9 of the additional CPR Practice Directions, to be inserted in the second practice direction (40B) to CPR Part 40 (judgments and orders):

'**14.4**   On any application or appeal concerning—
(i)   a committal order;
(ii)   a refusal to grant habeas corpus or
(iii)   a secure accommodation order made under section 25 of the Children Act 1989, if the court ordering the release of the person concludes that his Convention rights have been infringed by the making of the order to which the application or appeal relates, the judgment or order should so state. If the court does not do so, that failure will not prevent another court from deciding the matter'.

The new FPR rule 10.26, to be inserted after FPR rule 10.25 as reproduced above, provides for the procedure governing the joining of the Crown in cases involving judicial acts. Rule 10.26 (4) — (17) provides for the notice procedure to be followed where there is a possibility of a declaration of incompatibility being granted.10.26 (18) — (21) provide for the notice procedure in cases involving judicial acts:

'**Human Rights Act 1998**
10.26   (18)   Where a claim is made under section 9(3) of the Human Rights Act 1998 in respect of a judicial act the procedure in paragraphs (6) to (17) shall also apply, but the notice to be given to the Crown:
          (a)   shall be given to the Lord Chancellor and shall be served on the Treasury Solicitor on his behalf; and
          (b)   shall also give details of the judicial act which is the subject of the claim and of the court that made it.
(19)   Where in any appeal a claim is made in respect of a judicial act to which section 9(3) and (4) of that Act applies –
          (a)   that claim must be set out in the notice of appeal; and
          (b)   notice must be given to the Crown in accordance with paragraph (18).
(20)   The appellant must in a notice of appeal to which paragraph (19)(a) applies—
          (a)   state that a claim is being made under section 9(3) of the Human Rights Act 1998; and
          (b)   give details of—
                 (i)   the Convention right which it is alleged has been infringed;
                 (ii)   the infringement;
                 (iii)   the judicial act complained of; and
                 (iv)   the court which made it.
(21)   Where paragraph (19) applies and the appropriate person (as defined in section 9(5) of the Human Rights Act 1998) has not applied within 21 days, or such other

period as the court directs, after the notice is served to be joined as a party, the court may join the appropriate person as a party.

(22) On any application or appeal concerning—

    (a)   a committal order;

    (b)   a refusal to grant habeas corpus or

    (c)   a secure accommodation order made under section 25 of the Act of 1989,

if the court ordering the release of the person concludes that his Convention rights have been infringed by the making of the order to which the application or appeal relates, the judgment or order should so state, but if the court does not do so, that failure will not prevent another court from deciding the matter."

The new FPR practice direction provides as follows:

'Allocation to Judges

3.   (1)   [relates to declarations of incompatibility.]

       (2)   the hearing and determination of a claim made under the Act in respect of a judicial act shall be confined in the high Court to a High Court Judge and in county courts to a circuit judge'.